SIMPLER
BY THE DOZEN

© Blue Collar Mind Publishing

Editor: Stephanie Siu
Internal illustrations: Jason Hommas
Layout design: Carlla de Moura

DEDICATION

I want to first express my love and gratitude to Grandma Nancy who begged me for years to write a book and told me she'd be the first person to buy it.

To my mom, for showing me the pleasures of motherhood, and telling me early on that I could be a writer.

To my fantastic kids: Alex, Gavin, Elise, Maya, Violet, Annora, Jude, Margot, Sail, and Bryn for enriching my life in so many ways, and for helping manage the house while mom worked on her book.

Finally, to my husband and lifelong teammate, Bryan. I am humbled daily by his passion, support, and vision for progress. He gives me courage and grace when I need it the most.

Thank you

"In a house with two kids, it seems we have stuff everywhere. Have you noticed kids are messy? Keeping a clean and organized house can feel like playing Jenga with raccoons. When I learned the Orr family has 10 kids, I thought the parents must keep their sanity by making the kids sleep in the back yard. There must be stuff strewn about everywhere. But NOW I know the secret. And in Simpler by the Dozen, you will learn what all parents need to know to get their home under control. Leilani Orr will take hold of your hand and walk you through each area of your home. Whether it is deciding what to do with toys and trinkets, or clearing room in your closet or calendar, Leilani has tips and routines to get you and your family on track."

— *Jody Maberry: Dad, World Traveler*

"Simpler by the Dozen gave me a behind the scenes view into what it takes to run an orderly home. Leilani will give you a realistic perspective on what it's like to manage a home as a mother of 10 children. She will make you laugh out loud and give you the confidence that yes, you can create order amidst chaos!"

— *Vicky Lashenko, Mompreneur, Wife*

"This book is a must read for anyone who needs to gain control over life's messes, big or small! Simpler by the Dozen is a quick, tongue-in-cheek read with real, long term solutions to clean up your home, life, parenting, and schedule. You will find yourself pulling this book out time and time again to remind yourself that you're in control!"

— *Vanessa Vazquez: 2nd Grade Teacher, Mom, Wife*

CONTENTS

FOREWORD

I'm obligated to warn you that this book contains some fraudulent information.

You see, I have first-hand knowledge of the author's backstory, having met her when she was 13 years old and been privy to her inner circle since. I know what she is like behind closed doors, how she treats people when nobody is documenting it, and what her closet actually looks like.

I can therefore state with unequivocal confidence that the book you're holding is *fraught with understatement.*

Don't let her self-deprecation and humility fool you. She is the real deal.

Having been married to the author for 18 years, I've watched her carve order out of the chaos that our 10 children (yes, 10 children) and I wreak on our home. She attacks the messes we create with joy and grace, if sometimes a little good-natured yelling.

To say this book was only about organizing would be a misrepresentation. It is the result of a lifetime growing up with 12 siblings, then raising 10 kids (plus one pig-headed husband).

I owe everything good in my life to the woman who runs our home. Every success I've had, every positive character trait our children possess, have the author's fingerprints on them. As I like to tell people, "Our home has a CEO that would make Apple and Microsoft jealous."

The author is not an "expert," guru, or saleswoman by any means. She is a bonafide, real-life warrior that battles the demons of disorganization and excess daily with an army of kids in tow.

This book began as a friendly wager between the author and myself. I agreed to lose 12 pounds if she could write a book in —wait for it — 90 days.

Anybody who has attempted to put pen to paper can attest to the impossibility. Clearly, I had the advantage in our bet. Yet my wife surprised us both by pulling it off — this between cooking, cleaning, home educating our kids, and the 47,000 other things required of a mother.

This book is full of practical ways she has found to bring order to our lives, while embracing its inevitable chaos. You will find no idealism or dogma here. There are no "quick fixes" or other attempts to gloss over life's messy reality. This book is as gritty and full of unexpected challenges as the author has experienced them.

I hope you enjoy this window into her mind. I can assure you there is much more than this small book can contain. While I would happily keep her all to myself, it would be at humanity's great loss.

I am confident the masses whose lives are ruled by entropy will find success with her methods. Yet, there is one accomplishment they will never achieve.

I am and always will be the greatest fan of her life.

— *Bryan Orr*

PREFACE

A few years ago, I overheard comments about whether or not someone's possessions "sparked joy." I remember thinking, "That's a practical way to decide whether to keep it." I quickly moved on and didn't give a second thought to who or what was sparking all this "sparking joy" conversation.

When I recently accepted my husband's challenge to write a book in 3 months, I was scared. I love writing, but I'm a novice. I was afraid to pick too deep of a topic. What if I got it all wrong, the words got printed, and five years down the road, I'm hiding my face in shame because I messed up (in writing!) something that was near and dear to my heart.

My husband, being the awesome guy that he is, gave me simple and wise counsel:

"Pick something true to you that doesn't require a depth of emotion, and just run with it."

That sounded like a safe place to start writing, but I was at a loss for what fit that bill. Then it hit me.

STUFF!

That was it! Dealing with it is near and dear to me, but not at a soul-deep level.

So I got started on my book.

I was scrolling through my Facebook feed just recently and reading posts after posts about how friends are organizing their drawers, folding this or that, and "sparking joy."

"Wait a minute, is this still going around?" I thought. "Am I missing a key element to cultural society right now?"

Yes, it turned out, I was. I went first to Google, and then Netflix. I watched an episode (or three) of Tidying Up, and thought, "I like this lady!"

Marie Kondo is cool, and definitely calmer than me. I certainly don't hold to the same level of precision to dress (have you seen her impeccable wardrobe, it's impressive; I'm over here usually trying to figure out if I like hipster, preppy, or just good ol fashioned bell bottoms and then end up combining the styles and feel like a walking fashion disaster), but I find I greatly relate to her mindset of simplifying.

My relationship with organizing started when I was young.

Growing up the fourth of 12 kids, life was fun, chaotic, and adventurous. Things about our family might have seemed strange at times, but we were happy. More than that, we felt secure.

When I say "secure," I don't mean we always wore bike helmets, followed safety rules, and marched behind my parents like 12 ducklings.

With so many of us to care for, we didn't always do things by the book. Yet I never felt more secure than when I was sleeping on a pull-out sofa with four of my siblings. I couldn't move even if I wanted to. We took up every bit of space on that mattress and slept like five peas in a pod.

Family (and cramped quarters), that was where my security came from.

My mother is an incredible woman who has sacrificed a lot

for her children. She was a wise parent, but never forgot how to have fun with us either.

I will say this, however... Mom and I are very different people. I'll give you an example.

One thing I really looked forward to as a kid were visits from Grandpa and Grandma. Even with 12 of us, my grandparents had a way of making each of us feel individually pampered.

Mom gave the announcement casually, though its effect on me would be huge. "Hey kids, grandpa and grandma are coming for a visit tomorrow. Let's decide what we're going to have for dinner and get a few chores done around here."

At 13 yrs old I knew our house was a bit of wreck. There was mismatched furniture, handprints and jam over the kitchen cabinets, wires hanging from the ceiling where we had started to install lights but never got around to finishing it, a slew of bicycles — some working and some piling up like a bicycle salvage yard. A few cobwebs hung eerily from the corners.

With less than 24 hrs to get the house whipped into shape, I assumed leadership over the younger (I didn't dare bark at the older ones) siblings I shared a room with, barking at them to clean up their areas.

And yes, nine of us girls really slept in one room.

Maybe I was slightly embarrassed about a few areas of the house, but mostly I just wanted to make the place more comfortable. Our house wasn't much to show off no matter how much cleaning we did, but we could still do something about the way we presented it.

At some point during this frantic cleaning, mom would stop

me and tell me not to stress about everything being perfect. "Pretending you are somebody you're not to impress people isn't healthy," she would say.

I knew she just wanted me to relax, but I didn't see anything wrong with tidying up. I wasn't putting up a facade, I really enjoyed doing it.

Mom thought I should work on my tone if I wanted people to care about tidying up as much as I did, and she was right.

I needed my mom back then, but I think she needed me, too.

—

Mom had a love-hate relationship with my insatiable need to clean and organize.

She started offering me a few dollars for cleaning out her closet or bedroom, which I did happily. It seemed like a win-win situation for both of us.

Where we ran into trouble is when she couldn't find that stack of papers she set on the counter earlier because another sibling or I had tossed it, thinking it was doodling paper.

In our defense, my mom had a habit of doodling on everything. How were we supposed to decipher between an essential document and random paper if there were squiggly lines all over it?

"Who threw out my menu and list, again?" I'd hear mother shout, and knew it was time to confess.

Even at an early age, minimizing junk was a part of who I am.

As a kid, it seemed reasonable to sleep with a lot of siblings in the same room, if not the same bed. Sharing clothes, shoes, space and time with others was my normal.

The idea of "personal space" was nonexistent. There was no such thing as my own stuff, my room, and rarely my own bed. I'd simply adjusted to not having much in general.

When I visited a friend's house, it felt strange seeing kids with their own bed, clothes and toys. I didn't think they had it better. It just wasn't the way I was used to living.

Being part of a big family, we all pitched in to clean the house. It made sense to me that the less clutter there

"Mom had a love-hate relationship with my insatiable need to clean and organize."

was, the less there would be to maintain. By the time I left home as a young adult, it was the most natural way for me to live and thrive.

When I got married at 19, the 900-square-foot, two bedroom, two bath rental my husband and I moved into seemed crazy spacious. When you've lived in a big dorm with eight sisters most of your life, even a small space you only had to share with one person seemed large in comparison.

It was a joy to set up that first home the way I wanted.

Bryan and I moved pretty quickly to another rental and then another, always looking for a better deal. Shortly after we became parents, we downsized to a 600-square-foot apartment. The extra savings allowed us to put a bigger down payment on our first mortgage. Sacrificing space for a short time seemed worth it for our next, more permanent move.

When it came time to buy, we decided on a cute, three

bedroom, two bath, corner lot fixer-upper that had been constructed in 1947. Our new-to-us home sported cool wooden walls and ceiling beams in one room, and a stone exterior wall — but the pleasant aspects of the house ended there.

We spent the next six months tearing up old carpet and tile, pulling exterior siding off the house, replacing the roof, installing new fixtures, and putting a fresh coat of paint on almost every surface.

By this time, we had a two-year old boy and I was pregnant with our second son.

Life was changing fast. While my husband started his own business, I got into the groove of being a homeschooling parent and stay-at-home mom. A few years slipped by and before we knew it, baby number five was on the way.

We were determined from the start to do the "big family" thing, and went right ahead growing our family early on.

You may be thinking, "I thought this book was about simplifying! What's simple about having a ton of kids?"

For us, the decision was based more on our positive experience being in and around large households. Growing up in a big family, I always knew I wanted a lot of kids, and my husband, who came from a family of four, agreed it would be a blessing.

We never discussed exactly how many kids we wanted, or how we planned on making it work. We knew that raising children was a serious responsibility, but that God would walk with us and give us what we needed along the way.

And He certainly has.

For six years, we enjoyed our first home, living in the town Bryan and I both grew up in.

Yet with five kids in tow and the desire to continue growing our family, we began to give serious thought to rural living. Our house back then sat on the corner of an intersection, which meant we were always concerned about letting our children run around outside unattended.

After some scoping around, we found a place we liked out in the country and bought seven acres. Instead of selling our house in town, we rented it out to increase our income.

Our new purchase out in the boonies came with a lot of space, but it was in the land, not the house that rested upon it.

The home space would prove a challenge, but one that Bryan and I were up to handling.

This book is my journey of making sense out of the various spaces and circumstances we've encountered through our lives. You will notice that this gritty "guide" does not contain a lot of specific how-to advice. Context matters, and few people I know need to clean up after 10 kids.

Instead, I modeled this book more like a friend sharing practical methods of simplifying (imperfections and all) that has worked well for our large family of 12.

After 18 years of changes, difficult choices, challenges embraced, and the learning we've done throughout, we now live in the country with 10 children, a Golden Retriever, two rabbits, and a more sizeable living space.

How we got here has been the adventure of a lifetime.

PANTRY & REFRIGERATOR
(And How to Plan Meals Accordingly)

When we first moved to the country, our new home in
the boonies needed work. The kitchen was made up of a few
dilapidated cabinets, countertops that were warped beneath
a visible roof leak, and a diamond-patterned linoleum floor
that had been ripped and torn in multiple places.

Three giant steps was all it took to walk the length of the
kitchen, breakfast nook, and sitting area. The shag-like
carpet in the living area was a color of mixed green, yellow,
and brown that you could only title, "Vomit."

It was the "fireplace" and mantle in the sitting area, however, that really scared the living daylights out of me. What was once white plastic veneer had been yellowed by years of exposure to nicotine and tobacco streaked across the surface.

Inside the fireplace where there should have been a pile of cozy, burning logs, sat a pile of crap that reeked of urine. Whether it was human or animal, I couldn't tell.

When we first looked at the place the realtor had warned us, "I wouldn't use that fireplace without checking to see if it's safe."

> **"I really just wanted to light that fireplace and send it all down to Hades."**

I really just wanted to light that fireplace and send it all down to Hades.

Three steps backward and I was once again in my soon-to-be "kitchen."

"Where would I even store food here?" I thought to myself. The cabinet space was minimal, the refrigerator was small, and there was no obvious pantry area.

I peeked around the corner where a rusted out washer and dryer were smashed next to each other, and spotted a small door. It opened onto two small "shelves."

Shelves generally function best when they are horizontally installed. These sad, neglected ones, sagging under the weight of humidity and more overhead roof leakage, hung at more of a 45-degree angle.

Below these shelves was a large opening to an air duct —

the return vent for the 20-year-old heating-and-cooling package unit.

I shut the door, hoping to find some other place for my pantry.

Horrified by what I'd seen so far but determined to face my fears, I opened another door next to the small refrigerator.

This time I found the water heater.

The floor was once again that lovely diamond-patterned linoleum, coated with years of grime, dust, and rusty water, sprinkled with rat turds and roach wings. There was also, amazingly, one large (horizontal) shelf. The wood was splintered and warped, but could be redeemed.

Closing the door to what seemed like the best bet for our pantry, I couldn't help thinking again, "What the heck are we doing moving out to this place?"

When we decided to try "country living," we were hoping for a more spacious piece of property for our kids to run around on, and to save money by renting out our first house in town. Now, staying in town was starting to sound pretty good. Forget giving up our normal life (with normal shelves) to "one day" build a house on our seven acre piece of serenity. Our "dangerous" corner property in town was looking better and better with every step I took in our new Double Wide in the country.

I'd thought our fixer-upper house from 1947 was bad, but this 1990 double wide trailer was another story.

I'll never forget what the realtor said the first time we toured our new property, "The master bedroom is quite spacious, and we're positive the entire place is free from termites."

That was the selling point of this house: a big bedroom and no termites.

"Oops, there's a big hole here in the floor of the bathroom. Y'all watch your step." exclaimed the realtor as we peered at the dilapidated tub.

Outside, the sun was just starting to set. I could hear birds singing in the trees and see sandhill cranes soaring gracefully overhead.

Looking to the distance, I saw a vast green landscape dotted with trees and cows, and a charming pole fence around the neighboring property. The evening sky was a magnificent piece of live art, with changing colors and clouds that morphed from puffy pillows to intense dragon heads.

There was a quietness I liked about this place. No sirens. No traffic.

I imagined our family pulling chairs up in a circle around a crackling fire pit while we watched the sunset every night.

Despite its challenges, I wanted this place to become our home.

Over the next four months, we had the inside nearly gutted. We slapped texture, kilz, and paint on every surface of the home, patched up anywhere that leaked, and knocked down walls to open up the space for our growing family.

We replaced every surface in the kitchen with cheap white cabinets and a couple lengths of prefabricated Formica countertops. With a little frugal ingenuity from Bryan, the cost for the "kitchen upgrade" came out to just $900.

There was little we could do about the pantry situation other than putting the shelves back upright and slathering the surfaces with Kilz and paint.

By the end of our work, it was still a trailer, but the smells, linoleum, old carpeting and leaks were gone. The place was at least livable, if a bit cramped, and it became our happy home for seven years.

Living there, I learned never to take pantry space for granted. It also taught me how to use what room I *did* have more efficiently.

> "One of the best ways to live well within limited space is to simply buy what you need and live in the present."

With the space available, I couldn't stock up for more than a week's worth of food at a time, and even then I had to play Tetris with our groceries to make everything fit.

With nine kids and us two adults at one point, even a week's worth of food was no joke.

I thought not being able to buy in bulk would be expensive, but I was wrong. One of the best ways to live well within limited space is to simply buy what you need and live in the present.

While you may be tempted to "buy for the future" when there is a great deal, or because "the sale is so amazing," I did just fine following my budget and meal plan without maxing out on sales.

I often remind myself, "We're in America where food is

plentiful. The sale will come back around, so don't worry your little Dutch head about it."

In fact, I believe not having extra space actually helped me save money.

I passed on many "deals" at the supermarket simply because I couldn't imagine where I'd find space to store the food. That meant skipping out on a lot of 'BOGO' Cheez-Its.

If you have the pantry space, by all means take advantage of a few good sales. In general, however, focus on buying what you need to get through a couple of weeks, and going through your pantry often as you would any other part of your home.

Living in that Double Wide, I would dream about going to the store and buying four gallons of milk at once, knowing that I would have a place to store it. Having that kind of luxury meant keeping the fridge as compact as possible.

The thing about refrigerator space is that it never feels like you have enough. Yet, when you go to clean the fridge out, its contents will take over the counters, island and even some of the dining table. So obviously, the space can hold a lot. It just needs to be organized, and often.

I remember when my kids were too young to rummage in the refrigerator. It was much easier to keep it tidy back then. Now that I have children old enough to help with cooking, baking, and putting groceries away, no amount of rearranging will survive a 17-, 14-, 13-, 11-, 10-, 8-, and 6-year-old for long.

The refrigerator can become quite the exciting place, between leftovers, funky bacteria growth — and why do we always have four random bottles of mustard?! Occasionally, you find produce that looks like it's been through a dehydrator, or worse.

Once, I found myself holding an object I could have sworn was a cucumber three weeks ago, but was looking more like a dehydrated baby rat.

It was enough to make me second guess the theories I was teaching in my homeschool science. I hadn't adopted Darwin's theory of Speciation before, but this cucumber was forcing me to rethink everything.

Upon further inspection, I concluded that cucumbers may evolve in their appearance, texture, and even flavor over time, but it was still a cucumber, which is part of the Cucurbitaceae family (also known as a gourd or cucurbit).

Whew!

I thought for a minute I would have to gather the kids and discuss speciation, but cucumbers stay cucumbers, so let's move along.

I recommend checking what you already have in your refrigerator be a part of your weekly pantry routine. The last thing you need is for your spouse to come home with a handful of fresh garlic bulbs when you already have three hiding behind the two (opened) tubs of sour cream in the fridge.

While you're in there looking for garlic, feel free to combine those two tubs of sour cream, too.

Boom. You just made room for that gallon of milk.

Before you head to the store, root around in your fridge. Combine all like items. Discard those expired salad dressings. Who needs 13 bottles of expired salad dressing?

You should also toss that yellowing broccoli, and if your carrots and celery are as flexible as Elastigirl (possibly the greatest animation of all time — but I digress) throw those to the rabbits or in the compost pile.

Finally, spark some joy in your fridge by wiping down the shelves and doors before you load the food you've taken out back in.

Giving your refrigerator space to breathe will also give you a clearer head for grocery shopping. No more guessing what you need to get. Turns out, we have plenty of garlic but are out of cheddar cheese. With a dozen people in the house, you may guess what is our most costly expenditure:

FOOD.

Yes, the amount of money we spend on food is, quite frankly, amazing. It doesn't feel wasteful either, because most of what I buy will get eaten one way or the other. Still, I have to rein that category in, or just going to the grocery store would nigh clear out our bank account.

QUICK TIPS:

1. Figure out the amount you have to spend on food per week or month.

2. Take stock of your pantry and refrigerator.

3. Create a menu for one week including a daily list of breakfast, lunch, dinner, and snacks.

4. After consulting pantry and fridge, make a list for every item you need from the store

    a. This eliminates the need to make multiple trips throughout the week, which will aid both your organization AND budget.

5. Don't feel pressured to go "all organic." While eating clean is nice, strictly organic for a dozen people definitely strains the budget. I choose a few to splurge on, like peanut butter, eggs, lettuce, and bananas.

6. At the store, remain true to the items on your list.

7. Don't shop for groceries when you're hungry.

8. Find ways to make homemade or more frugal snacks.

9. Limit snack times and attempt to structure how the kids forage your pantry.

The pantry and fridge are what I call "maintenance spaces." I encourage you to revisit them often to prevent excess and waste. The pain of throwing out food can be just the motivation you need to buy smarter and only keep on hand the groceries you need for this week.

It's not that I'm against buying in bulk (I utilize wholesale grocery stores for certain items), or making "freezer meals" like generations of big families have done before me. However, these "stock up" techniques don't always make sense considering the extra space they require.

[2]

KITCHEN

Back when Bryan and I first got engaged, I was 18 and he was 17. Can you believe that one of the prerequisites my parents had to receive their blessing for marriage was that we wait until Bryan was 18? Like every teenager or young adult, we thought, "We're so mature and capable, what could go wrong?!"

One of the last special moments I had with my dad before I left home was sitting down with him one afternoon to go over what it would look like for Bryan and I to live on our own.

On old-school pen and paper, my dad and I went over the costs of everything a newlywed couple would need to live.

The budget we came up with covered just the basics. It didn't include extras like cable, internet, cell phones (this was before we relied on smartphones for everything), eating out, or vacations. It wasn't going to be a flashy start, but we came up with an amazingly low dollar number.

My dad and I were both excited at the result. By the looks of it, moving out was going to be surprisingly affordable.

When I brought the budget to Bryan, he was excited too. It solidified how we could make it on our own. If we didn't do anything crazy, we would be just fine. This exercise with my dad also gave me a strong sense early on of "needs" vs. "wants."

While we never had to live quite that frugally, we always knew that it was feasible, at least on paper. And that level of extreme minimalism always held a sense of adventure to me. Sure, it means denying ourselves a lot of things, but also gaining the freedom of knowing that we don't need everything we think we do.

This brings us to the most important, and often most cluttered room in any house.

If you've ever moved from one place to another, you might have noticed one room that always requires a crazy amount of boxes to clear out.

If you thought of the KITCHEN, you're not alone. Bryan and I have moved six times throughout our married life, and each time, that room seems to have the most amount of boxes to pack.

I get it. We eat 3-10 times a day. Still, it's always shocking how much stuff accumulates in that space, especially when the process of eating seems so simple. Get food, prep food, eat food. Wash the dishes and you're done.

I've never been one for fancy gadgets and tools — even when it means I sometimes do things harder, not smarter. That "minimalist" mindset has served us well when space was very limited, or we had a tight budget.

Bryan and I have lived in a few different homes, and I've found that no matter how much or little space we have in them, the kitchen always gets filled up. (This is partly because Bryan likes having all the gadgets and tools to make the job easier.)

Kitchens are the focal points of many living spaces. Even if you don't like to cook, it seems we're always in there for one reason or another. That means many kitchens end up being a 'catch-all' spot for various things that don't have a home anywhere else in the house.

No matter how much space you have, it's important to go through your kitchen often and downsize as much as possible. Every now and then, I like to sort through my kitchen by category, starting with cups and glasses.

It's ridiculous how many free plastic cups we accumulate.

If you have children, I dare you to go and count all of the plastic cups you didn't buy. Then get a trash bag and give away half of them. If your house is anything like mine, just doing that will free up significant cabinet space.

I usually end up tossing almost all the free plastic cups we get from fast food Kid's Meals or were handed out at a convention. Extra cups are useful, but we don't need them taking up four shelves of precious kitchen space. You can stack them to high heaven, but the 29 Ollie the Olive Kid's Meal cups is starting to reach "hoarding" level.

After a few days of use, take the liberty to recycle the free cups your kids took home with them.

The plastic cups are the easy part. Then there are sippy cups. And coffee mugs. And wine glasses. The fact that you can't stack wine glasses is painful. You can fit maybe six of them on a shelf before you're out of space for anything else.

A friend of mine recently bought a house nearby, and mentioned that their home was blanketed in moving boxes that she hadn't unpacked.

Some weird neurological spark went off in my brain when she mentioned, "moving boxes." I jumped at the chance to help make her new home warm and livable, and immediately offered to sort those boxes with her.

"Ohhhhh, may I come help?" I asked, watching her eyes light up.

My friend Nora is witty, smart and a great conversationalist. Best of all, she laughs both *with* and *at* me, which is basically a love language in the Orr household.

Forget the "receiving gifts" love language — that just leads to more stuff. We prefer the sixth love language: jokes and sarcasm.

Nora's a thinker AND a doer.

Anybody who meets Nora can't help but like her.

A few days after our conversation, I went over for our box-emptying rendezvous.

The first step I take with any unpacking or organizing project is to set back, take in all the boxes, and scope out the area.

Nora had about six or seven cabinets and three drawers for all her kitchen accoutrements (fancy word, eh?). This is no joke. If you think your kitchen is small, I bet hers is smaller.

This situation was especially unique for another reason: Nora is a sentimental collector—her words, not mine!

Not only does she hold onto things for nostalgic reasons, she'll often keep them just in case she might need it later.

Here we were together, one sentimental collector and a happy declutterer.

Nora gets some credit here. The fact that she wanted my assistance proved she was ready to let some things go. Nora knows I cherish our relationship. Yet we both knew when it comes to organizing, that shirt from middle school or any other sentimental trinkets won't mean much to me.

That's if we ever finish with the boxes for the kitchen.

Whatever year Nora's house was constructed, the builders did not consider that its 2019 occupants might have more than one plate, one mug, one pot, and two mixing bowls.

"Here we were together, one sentimental collector and a happy declutterer."

We unwrapped all the kitchen goodies, and then the fun began.

I have to say, the number of wine glasses Nora owned got me thinking that my friend just might be a lush.

As we went through glass after glass, Nora told me the story of each one and why they should have a place in the cabinet.

A lot of them weren't even items Nora had picked out herself, but gifts from her mother, friend, or great-great-Aunt Josephine from the Galapagos Islands.

When we looked at how much space Nora had compared to the size of her glass collection, it was clear that some of them had to go.

As I held up mug after mug, Nora would shake her head, or nod thoughtfully when we came across one she couldn't live without.

The "Yard Sale" bin filled up fast as she got more comfortable letting go. We kept enough wine glasses to share a drink when company was over and tossed the rest. (Ahem, have I mentioned "lush"?)

We went through the same process with her mixing bowls, casserole dishes, plates, and baking sheets. Nora was determined to make her new home functional, comfortable and (mostly) clutter-free.

My favorite part was sorting through the kitchen tools. Believe it or not, Nora only had one drawer to fit all of her utensils and silverware.

When you have three can openers, and only two adults, you realize the utensil-to-people ratio might be off. We kept one and put the other two in the "Yard Sale" container. We kept going this way with the spatulas (keep two, toss three), soup ladles (keep one, toss one), and whisks (same, same). For silverware, we kept just enough for a setting of four people.

If you're trying to declutter kitchen knives, keep a few of your favorites, then aim the rest at a big tree trunk and see how skilled you are at cutlery flinging. You know, just in case you're in the wild one day and a bear with rabies starts chasing you. It's good to be prepared for such things.

The morning at Nora's morphed into the afternoon. Her kitchen was now functional, and all the necessities (plus a few extra) were neatly tucked away into cabinets and drawers.

At this point, the trash cans were full, and the giveaway bins overflowing. We stopped for lunch before tackling the boxes labeled "Living Room" and "Miscellaneous." By late afternoon we had gone through most of the boxes AND finished setting up the living, dining, and kitchen areas.

The amount of organizing we got done in just 6 hours, even with a lunch and coffee break, felt productive and rewarding. And most of this was accomplished because of Nora.

Every item passed through her. She made the decision of what to do with them. Nora was aware of her own "sentimental attachment" and what objects she was holding onto out of guilt, or to spare "Aunt Josephine's" feelings.

Many of us have an "Aunt Josephine." She might even be our mother, but if the puke green floral patterned ceramic bowl isn't working in your space, "Bye, bye ceramic bowl."

To maintain your space (and your sanity), it's essential not to let other people's emotions control how you function in your own home.

Remember, it's just stuff, and it's good to hold loosely.

There's no reason to be mean-spirited, but they're your things, and you have the right to do what's best with them.

It's easy for kitchen items to unknowingly pile up, like when I lose my favorite wooden spoon, and buy another one to replace it. Of course, as soon as I do that, my old one shows up, my spouse also bought one, the kids bring in two from the sandbox outside, and now I have five.

Stuff like that happens all the time, which is why I make a habit of going through our kitchen regularly. In fact, I may go sift through a drawer or two right now, 'cause I better practice what I preach.

Simplicity in the kitchen is much like simplifying any other space. The first step is learning to give up the nonessentials.

Hiding clutter behind cabinet doors is not a solution to enriching your life. If you're having trouble letting go, try picturing glass doors on all of your storage space. There's nowhere for your things to hide. Use that imagery to guide what you keep and what can go.

Be brave! Embrace the challenge to tackle clutter by tossing what you don't need. No matter how long it takes, don't give up on your project until you've made it through the entire kitchen.

Approach it the same way you would eat an elephant:

Don't try to swallow it whole. Just take one bite at a time until it's gone.

QUICK TIPS:

1. Your kitchen is no place for gifts and gadgets that you don't use regularly.

2. Don't allow the monsters of disorganization to hide behind cabinet doors.

3. If you want to tidy up your house, start in the kitchen. It'll be fun to watch the junk disappear before your eyes, and you'll be astonished at how much easier it will be to find everyday items afterwards.

[3]

CLOSETS

A common misconception people have is thinking "My organizational problems would be solved if I had more closet space!" In reality, closets can pose a real threat to your organizational ambitions. That's because closets have doors, and doors hide things. A whole lot of awful, wretched things.

"Who wants to clean my closet? I'll pay you $5!" I remember my dear mother calling to the house at large.

Back in the 90's, $5 was a lot to a 13 year old. That could buy you a 64 ounce Thirst Buster, a mini pack of Oreos, AND a small bag of Doritos at the local gas station.

I immediately raised my hand and my voice. You had to be both quick AND loud when you were one of 12 kids.

"And the opportunity goes to the brown haired teen with messed up bangs."

I'd race down the hall to claim my prize.

My family's house growing up was...unique. Its original frame was 70 years old, with more recent front and back wings added on. The guy who remodeled definitely wasn't fond of closets; the entire house had just one. It was a large walk-in that all the kids and our parents shared.

It was no joke, this closet.

Do you remember the wardrobe in Narnia where the kids enter and the coats just sort of swallowed them up?

Well, my mom's closet was similar, except there was nothing magical on the other side.

All four walls had racks of hanging clothes. On the top level of racks and above were piles of folded clothes stacked so high that they often toppled over onto the floor.

> **"Closets have doors, and doors hide things. A whole lot of awful, wretched things."**

Squished among the folded clothing were shoes and a few random items. And above those folded garments was yet another level of racks with more hanging clothes.

But the most terrifying part of this closet was neither the racks or the shelves. It was the floor.

What lay underneath the hanging clothes, or was simply

strewn about, felt like a mountain of questions waiting to be solved.

Now you know why my mom was willing to pay for someone to take that chore.

While I worked hard to restore order to that room, any cleaning I did was only a temporary fix. It never stayed that way for long, and how could it with 14 of us?

My family is a hard-working, capable bunch, but the idea of "not making a mess" was lost on us. Everyone seemed to operate on a default setting of 'leave it on the floor and deal with it later.'

This room was a recurring problem throughout my childhood. I learned that closets can easily become terrible, frightening, no good, horrible places.

As an adult, and more importantly a parent, I've developed a system for keeping closets clean.

Not unlike my childhood, there have been times that our closet space was extremely limited. We did the best we could with simple shelving and bins for specific items to aid in organization. Mostly it just came down to going through our things often, and making sure we weren't holding onto anything unnecessary.

If you guys think our wardrobes are always organized, please put this book down for a second and know in the deepest part of your soul that we, like everyone else, have issues with our closets.

But when they're cleaned and things are put away correctly, everything fits.

And that's the primary goal.

So how do you do that?

Some people like to ask, "Does it spark joy?" about objects in their home. I would rather use the darker, "Is it a silent killer?" approach.

I like to begin by going into the closet with a large trash bag or bin and taking a moment to just stare at everything. Then I'll start parsing through clothes, Christmas ornaments, and shoes that no longer add enough value to justify holding onto them.

One helpful tool is to look at almost every piece of clothing and think, "When's the last time the kids or I wore that?" Unless it's a seasonal or formal piece, anything that hasn't been worn in more than 6 months gets the bin.

This next part is crucial. After making my decision, I'll put the unwanted item in the bag and won't question it for another second. It's over. Outta sight, outta mind.

Once I start tossing clothes, it feels freeing to take material items and realize they're not needed in my life. Next thing you know, I have at it with all kinds of stuff.

Pretty soon, I'll have a bag or two of things to take to Goodwill, and an organized closet that is no longer a "silent killer" but a blessing of clean storage space.

The more frequently I organize the closet, the quicker and more natural it becomes.

If you're anything like me, having an organized closet even for 30 minutes is a huge accomplishment and moment to celebrate in the journey of parenthood.

Some people may prefer to schedule a day for closet cleaning, say once every three months, or twice a year. Few of us are actually that structured. It's

> **"Closets can easily become terrible, frightening, no good, horrible places."**

enough to just be more aware. You can make tidying up a regular routine without having to put it on the calendar.

Don't forget: the less you have, the easier it is to clean. That means the first time might be a chore, but every time after that should get easier.

QUICK TIPS:

1. Hold on to less clothes.

2. Go through your stuff regularly. Make sure everything has a designated place, and don't keep more than you have reasonable space for.

3. Take joy in the limited windows of "closet perfection." Even if you don't maintain a spotless closet all the time, knowing that your space has the ability to house everything you own neatly is a good feeling.

[4]

GARAGE OR NO GARAGE

If you have a garage, I'm a little jealous of you right now.

My entire adult life, I've only lived somewhere with a garage once, and we were there for 9 months.

That means I've rarely had the luxury of that extra room outside the house to stash things.

In some ways, this has forced me to be better about not collecting junk.

My husband, well, that's another story.

One day I opened the mailbox and found a yellow slip from

the post office inside. The box next to "Package too large to deliver" was checked.

"No biggie," I thought. I'll just run down to the post office and pick it up on my next grocery store trip.

Inside that dank, institutional, government building called USPS, I walked up to the counter where a man named "Jim" helped me.

"I'm here to pick up a package that was 'undeliverable due to size,'" I told him.

"Yeah, so about that…" he said. "By law, I'm not even supposed to accept packages over 100 pounds here at this post office."

Hmmm, so not only was this package big, it was heavy.

"Do you have a large vehicle to haul the package in?" Jim asked. "Also, I presume you're going to need help loading it, but like I said, I'm not legally allowed to accept or even assist you with this size of a package."

Now I'm wondering what the heck Bryan ordered.

How big, exactly, was this thing? I have no recollection of us ordering something that would require multiple adults to maneuver, or why would we even need it.

Oh geez, and where was Bryan planning to even store this thing?

I'm starting to get a little ticked. Stuff can be fun, but it can also get in the way, and make me kinda mad.

On our seven acre property in the country, we have this rinky-dink, rat-infested shed crammed with fold-up tables, camping supplies, the riding lawn mower lift, outdoor games, insulated coolers, weed eater, leaf blower, pole saws, chain saws, rakes, shovels, ripsticks, the kids' scooters, tarps, a stupid amount of field cones and flags, and — for some reason — 28 cans of WD-40.

That shed hurts me. To my deepest inner soul. As many times as I've tried to organize it, it ends up being a massive game of Tetris just to fit it all in. I go through that thing regularly, but it's never enough. Just this past "shed clean-out" session, I filled seven bins full of things I couldn't justify keeping in hopes of bringing order to this chaotic space.

> **"Now I was starting to get a little ticked. Stuff can be fun, but it can also get in the way, and make me kinda mad."**

I've tried to get my family to care about how things are put away in there, but it's hard to get around the amount of objects we have to fit in there, and the work it takes to get anything out. It poses a problem even for me, let alone my 14 year old boy and nine other kids who couldn't care less what the shed looks like.

As you can see, there are genuine storage issues even for people like me who don't collect junk.

So there I am at the post office wondering what in tarnation could be in this box that Jim can't hand off to me.

Bryan, Bryan, Bryan, why do you do this to me?

"Where should I pick it up?" I asked Jim.

"Just back up to the loading dock behind the main building and y'all can have at it," he said.

I walked out to the van and looked inside at my nine kids. Unfortunately, my oldest wasn't with us.

"Um, I'm going to need your help. We gotta lift some big box and make it fit in here, so let's get this done."

I drive behind the building. It felt like a scene from a movie, where I'm sneaking around to some back area to pick up illegal substances or something crazy like that. Meanwhile the back sensor on my van is going off (loudly) as I back up to the loading ramp. Very subtle indeed.

Three of the kids and I hop out. The USPS employee had this dubious look on his face, like he's wondering how we were going to attempt this.

We climbed up to the loading dock to tackle a box bigger than all three of us while the employee just stood there awkwardly watching.

The box was unmarked, which made the whole thing seem even creepier. Somehow, the kids and I got the package into the van. Thank heavens for extended height and extended length — we needed both for this delivery.

I thanked Jim, shut the van doors — there was 1/16th of an inch to spare — and we headed home.

We were going grocery shopping, but now we had zero space for anything else. The store would have to wait while we made a detour to drop this package off at home.

You may be wondering why I didn't just text Bryan and tell

him he can get his own package from the post office. I could have, but then I'd be just as inefficient as USPS.

Bryan was likely working, or *ahem* golfing. Besides, procrastinating a chore annoys me almost as much as our rinky-dink, rat infested, full-to-the-brim shed. *Almost.*

I know the suspense is killing you by now. What was in the package?

It was a subwoofer speaker the size of a small house.

With a dozen of us living in the country on seven acres of grass and woods, we loved throwing huge parties and get-togethers at our house. To do that, we needed equipment.

We were hosting an outdoor New Year's Eve party in a few weeks. About 120 guests were expected to come, so OF COURSE Bryan projected we needed a speaker that could be heard across the entire county.

After opening that box, I rolled my eyes to the moon, and back, about 23 times.

Long after the party ended, that thing still doesn't have a proper home. Like I said, it was practically the size of a small house.

We still just have one rinky-dink shed, so the subwoofer is sitting outside on our covered porch until we finish building a garage this year to fit it.

Yes. We're building an entire garage, just to fit that subwoofer.

The point of this story was to illustrate that not having a garage for certain things is tough, but we've found ways to make it work.

Usually, that begins with not having those things in the first place.

If Bryan gets an urge to buy something that won't fit in the house, I remind him that it will most likely have to stay outside and be subjected to the elements.

Some things we end up buying anyway, like our bicycles, which end up decaying on the lawn. Luckily, I planned ahead. Knowing they will get ruined anyway, we buy all our bikes used or cheap.

Bryan and I are usually on the same page about keeping clutter on the downside. However, he's also a nerd and always on the lookout for the right tool to accomplish whatever project he's working on.

The fact that sometimes the perfect tool is a massive subwoofer, well, just kinda pains my brain.

If you're a garage owner, what do you have in there? Is it a place for a car? Or is that just an amusing joke—who has space to keep a vehicle in their garage?

Garages are a lot like closets. They can be horrifying. And they have doors. As we now know, when you have doors, you can hide things. But as with any dedicated space, they can also be ridiculously awesome and useful.

When I get a garage, it will be a designated space for storing specific things.

A garage doesn't need to become a junk collector's paradise. Unless you own a salvage yard and make money buying and selling scraps. Then, well, I won't argue with that.

Make room for your car. I dare you.

QUICK TIPS:

1. The more space you have, the more overwhelming it can become to organize if you allow the area to fill up with nonessentials.

2. Don't allow your garage to become a catch-all for the junk you clear out from other areas in your home. If you clean out the kitchen, but store the extra junk in the garage, that's not really simplifying. You're just moving trash around.

3. Having a garage can be useful. Don't take it for granted! Use the space for large items that need protection from the elements, and maybe even give yourself a work table to 'nerd-out' on a project now and then. You should enjoy this extra storage space.

NEEDS VS. WANTS

Making spaces work for you is about honing in on the right mindset, and knowing the difference between needs vs. wants is a huge factor.

When I can decipher between needs and wants, I am forced to realize how blessed I am. Many of us are living with an abundance of stuff and don't even recognize how lucky we are.

There is often an emotional/spiritual attachment we have with our things. I'm mostly going to address the practical and logical side of how separating needs and wants will help free up space in your heart and your home.

With any space you're trying to organize, simply look at each item and ask yourself: need or want?

I'm not saying 'wants' are a terrible thing, or that you should toss them all immediately. However, asking yourself which one it is can help clarify something as basic as how many t-shirts to hold onto.

For example, I have 35 t-shirts.

I 'need' three t-shirts.

I 'want' 15 t-shirts.

I can ditch the other 20.

And if you 'want' all 35 t-shirts, that's entirely up to you. However, if you also 'want' to declutter and free up your space, you will have to make sacrifices somewhere.

Distinguishing between needs and wants will help you determine where your priorities are, which can help answer the question of whether to buy or keep something, and where to put it.

I want to make one thing clear: I'm not a true minimalist.

I like stuff, nice stuff. I also like to buy and keep stuff.

But no matter how nice your things are, when they start to permeate and take over your house, they become more burdensome than helpful or fun.

> **"I have 35 t-shirts. I *need* three t-shirts. I *want* 15 t-shirts. I can ditch the other 20."**

Sometimes we have needs, but put a lot of entitlement and 'want' around them.

Take my teenagers, for instance. Last week, one of them

copped an attitude about how they only wanted a particular brand of a hoodie. He told me he "couldn't stand" the one he had, and wasn't gonna wear it anymore.

I took the hoodie he complained about (it was a nice one) and gave it to someone else who would appreciate it more. When my teen found out, he said, "Where's my hoodie? Now I don't have any hoodies to wear!"

I laughed — not in a jovial way, more of a "sorry, buddy" chortle — then shrugged.

"If I recall correctly, you said you won't wear that kind anymore, so I made sure it will be put to better use elsewhere."

Then I told him he can buy his own hoodies from now on.

You may think that's harsh, but that's what being a caring parent can mean sometimes.

And you know what?

My teen apologized to me (eventually) and now happily wears the "uncool" hoodies that I buy. Faced with the reality of having to spend their own money, clothes take on a different priority for young people.

Plus, that rotten entitled attitude is ugly even to a teen's ears — just give them space to hear it themselves.

We all have needs and wants, but often we get them confused.

In this case, the hoodie was a need, and the brand name was a want. Learning to differentiate between them does double duty for parenting and tidying up.

I buy a certain amount of clothes for my teens. If they want more, or anything name brand, they can wait to get them as gifts or until I find a good sale. Otherwise, they can buy their own. Getting your teens to pick up a job helps in the parenting department, too. They learn responsibility, and it takes the burden off you to buy every little thing their hearts desire.

Recognizing the difference between needs and wants not only guides whether I buy something in the first place, but also what I do with the item through its lifetime.

It's easy to make up exotic excuses why we need this or that consumer product. Sometimes it even seems like an infectious disease of American culture. In reality though, all that stuff does little for our overall happiness.

QUICK TIPS:

1. Keep in mind the only things we really "need" are food, water, shelter, and a handful of clothes.

2. Everything else are choices that we have the liberty to control. These extras can aid us, ease our pain, or give us pleasure, but they also have the ability to overwhelm and create stress—the opposite of what we intended!

3. Learn to appreciate these extras as the luxuries they are. You'll enjoy them more, and likely consume more responsibly. Bonus: If you have kids, they will benefit from that mindset as much as you do.

[6]

DECLUTTERING YOUR SCHEDULE AND LEARNING TO SAY NO

What is your relationship with the word "no"?

Usually, when you say "no" to someone, you get a reaction of some kind.

They may be surprised that you would turn them down, or else sad because you're the 'life of the party' and are denying an invitation. Their reaction may be even darker: pity, confusion, judgment, or a misunderstanding.

One of the liberties I've taken as I've gotten older is allowing myself to say no more often and choosing not to give in to guilt, either self-induced, or from other social or societal pressures.

Let me tell you, it's been awesome. Learning to say no isn't just about saving space in your home and closet, it's about pursuing order and minimizing stress as well.

> **"It was easier to be carefree with just two. Now that we were adding a newborn, my parenting methods needed more structure"**

While I am on the extroverted side, it's been a while since I was the '23-year-old mom of two' who had to be at every event. My '37-year-old mom of 10' life now looks very different.

As a younger, stay-at-home mom with a handful of kids, I had my household routines, but also found plenty of time to stay connected with my girlfriends, sisters, and parents. In fact, I had a blast toting around our two boys in search of adventure.

My parents were always welcoming. Anytime I dropped in, the kids would tear around and play, while I caught up with the family, then we'd head home in time for naps.

Life was simple, but time flies when you're having fun.

One day you wake up and realize your kids aren't just babies anymore. There are things they need to learn. These little people under your care actually need adult guidance. Imagine that!

It was easier to be carefree with just two. Now that we were adding a newborn however, my parenting methods needed more structure.

I was homeschooled from kindergarten through 12th grade and loved it. Before we even had kids, Bryan and I planned on homeschooling our children as we both had been. When our first kid was 3 ½ yrs old, I was already absorbing everything I could about teaching preschool and had started taking the next steps to homeschool seriously.

Bryan and I attended a homeschool convention together, which got us excited about the journey of home education. We began discussing our "whys" and beliefs about academics. Then we put our thoughts and ideas together, and chose various curriculums to use with our kids.

I took naturally to my new role as a homeschooling parent. After all, I was homeschooled throughout the entirety of grade school. *However,* "being a homeschooled kid" and "homeschooling my own kid" are two very different things.

I would second guess myself plenty, and often wondered if I was the worst mom and teacher ever. To be honest, my oldest is about to graduate high school, and I *still get those feelings of self-doubt.*

Whether you're a beginner homeschooler, or a seasoned veteran those feelings of inadequacy may be here to stay.

However, you're in charge of those hours in your day, which means learning to make decisions and prioritize.

Sometimes that means realizing you are responsible for more than just you, and denying yourself time to do something you might enjoy more.

There are a lot of events, engagements, and expectations from the outside world I've chosen to turn down. Don't get me wrong, I still love a good party, so please keep sending me your invites!

The point is that prioritizing may not always be fun, but is an essential measure to take in the pursuit of order amidst chaos.

As a homeschooling parent of *many kids,* one of the choices I've had to make was saying "no" to homeschooling co-ops. Ironic, I know.

These co-ops are groups of homeschooled kids and their parents who meet regularly for group lessons. Adults with a particular expertise can pick subjects they want to teach the group, just like teachers in school would specialize. Throughout the week, children and their parents do homework for that subject at home and bring their work to "class" once a week to share.

The concept is interesting, but here are a few reasons I've chosen to opt out:

1) With 10 kids in multiple grades, it would be hard to find a co-op that can accommodate all of them.

2) These co-ops usually want parents to volunteer and participate as much as possible. I'm usually tied to a nursing infant and at least one or two toddlers, which makes it difficult to find, much less coordinate, the blocks of time needed to focus on these group classes.

3) Even if I picked a simple role like "babysitter," I'd almost need someone to watch the other kids I have at home while I was babysitting at the co-op, which sounds ridiculously inefficient to me.

4) The extra time it takes to do assignments for every subject in preparation for the group class doesn't seem worth it.

5) Attending the co-op meetings breaks up my regular routine, and would likely be the only thing I get done that day.

6) I also live in the country, and the benefits do not justify an hour long round-trip commute.

I had to weigh these drawbacks against considerable pros:

1) It could be a lot of fun for the kids and me.

2) The children could benefit from learning more about a subject I wasn't passionate or knowledgeable about.

3) It's an opportunity to socialize, especially with other homeschooling parents and kids.

4) A lot of my homeschooling friends have good things to say about it.

Saying "no" hasn't always been easy, especially to something you have never tried and may enjoy if you did. Co-ops are a great option for many homeschoolers that, for my own reasons and schedule, I've chosen not to participate in.

I may decide to at some point, but when and if is my call.

Another common question I get asked is: are your kids involved in organized sports?

I want you to stop for a minute and consider the time and coordination (and money) it takes to involve two kids in sports. Then I want you to multiply that by five.

In short, year-round organized sports are not a regular routine of ours.

During the summer we've participated in golf camps

> **"Better that your choices give you wings to fly than leave you drowning in indecision."**

that are more conducive to our schedule. Plus, golf is a sport that runs in the family, so it's been fun to have the kids learn the focus and discipline of that particular sport and participate with other kids doing the same.

Don't get me wrong, we do enjoy sports and competition, but as for typical organized sports year round, this is another area we've kept it "simpler by the dozen" and have said "no."

However, we have a great community for freestyle, laid back athletic games and our kids get plenty of chance to "get on the field and play their hearts out" without having to "officially sign up".

They seem to be developing just fine without the typical after school sports.

Part of taking control, of both your life and living spaces, is not being pressured into things that don't work for you.

QUICK TIPS:

1. Being decisive will make life easier to manage. You won't always choose perfectly, but that's okay. Better that your choices give you wings to fly than leave you drowning in indecision.

2. Remember that saying 'no' to one thing means saying 'yes' to something else.

3. When you're faced with something cluttering your schedule, try saying 'no' and see where it takes you.

[7]

CLOTHES

It's a nice feeling when you can put on a nice outfit and get your kids looking sharp before heading out into the public. Most of the time, my kids look like country bumpkins, but they easily transform into cute preppy kids with just a few well-chosen articles.

Not that there's anything wrong with looking like a country bumpkin.

Clothes, while fun, also take up a crazy amount of space, easily wreaks havoc on my budget, can get ridiculously out of order, and cause heartache in both storage and laundry.

Here's the thing: you don't need a lot of clothes. In fact, the more we have, the harder it is to find anything. This is especially true for my younger kids who are learning to be more independent, and create a mess every time they have to pull out clothes or put them away.

Then there's the issue of storage. It doesn't matter whether you have the space to lay your clothes out neatly, or have endless closets in which to hang them up or not, because with 10 kids, it's always a juggling act between staying true to organization and making sure the kids are dressed well, regardless.

Almost every chapter in this book involves some kind of "just say no" moment. You might even call it an indirect lesson of minimalism.

Has anything like the following happened to you before?

You pull out your phone and check your email. Four new emails from Old Navy, Gap, The Children's Place, Target — wow, 50% off every item in store!

"Well, it has been a while since I've bought jeans for..." I'll start thinking.

STOP!

Before you start buying more clothes, go clean out the kids' closets and dressers. After that, climb to the attic, go out to the garage, dig into the deepest, darkest, saddest, most depressing part of your closets and pull out the clothes you have saved there.

Then finish laundering the 41 loads of dirty clothes in the laundry room.

After you went through all of the above, you may be

surprised by what you actually need, and what you didn't know you already had.

Don't make the mistake of shopping blind. I've bought things for one kid that had plenty, while another of my kids genuinely needed something. Epic fail.

When you've pulled out all the clothes you have stashed or lost in every crevice of the house, you may realize that much of it holds no real value to you any longer.

You already know what I want you to do with it.

Purge.

Many people hold onto clothes to avoid being wasteful, but they aren't helping you or anybody else just sitting in your attic. Sort through the pile for anything in decent shape that is useful for you and then and give the others away to someone who will wear them.

And you know that Target brand t-shirt Johnny outgrew 5 years ago? The one with stains all down the front from when he was teething? You can put that one in the trash without hesitation.

Trust me, it wasn't worth holding on to.

It was from Target.

There are 50 of the exact same one at the consignment store down the road.

For Pete's sake, there's mildew on it.

Nobody needs that shirt.

Put it in the trash.

Don't underestimate how junk clutters your mind as well as your home space.

Our household tries to function with a minimal amount of clothing. That means by the time our kids outgrow something, it's gotten so much use that it isn't usually worth passing down.

I do love when a quality jacket, outfit or pair of shoes can be handed down to another child. However, clothes have a limited lifespan, so that isn't always possible.

What the heck are we doing with five bins of spare clothes when we don't even remember what's in them?

I limit myself to 1-2 medium bins for the saved baby clothes and various sizes of hand me downs, and will check them regularly.

We live in a time when consignment stores are plentiful and even new clothes are affordable on sale. Given the current economy, I don't see the need to hoard unnecessary baggage.

> **"As far as I'm concerned, darning my socks means I've sent them to hell."**

There may have been a time and place to hoard clothes, like when people darned their own socks. Here in the 21st century, I couldn't even tell you what that means. As far as I'm concerned, darning my socks means I've sent them to hell.

So, the next time your unread emails scream "SALE," remember that the same deals will come around again in a month or two. Unless you're looking to buy something specific, feel free to delete those messages without even opening. Now enjoy your clutter-free inbox and dresser drawers.

Let me stop for a minute and talk about *hand-me-downs.*

For some reason, having a large family seems to summon the generosity of other people and before you know it, we end up with two or three black garbage bags full of free clothes.

Sometimes it's AWESOME. The clothes are often in great condition, and it saves me a trip to shop for 12 people.

You know what else?

It can sometimes be exactly what I *don't* need.

In a case like this, I let myself be "picky," taking just a few items that we'd appreciate, and passing the rest on. By 'a few items' I mean I usually keep 10%, if that. So in a bag of fifty pieces, I might keep five. There, I just did some math for ya.

Less is more, and real freedom is often just saying no and letting go.

One way to gauge if we're piling absurd amounts of clothing is when the designated storage areas for any of the kids become difficult to manage.

We've had different arrangements over the years, but we typically have a few dressers with each kid getting two drawers for their clothes. If those drawers have clothing spilling out because they're packed to bursting (and not just messy!) then it's time to purge.

There are a lot of different storage methods you can use for clothes: from boxes to bins, and hangers to hooks on the wall. I love when people come up with unique ways to store clothes that works best for the space they're in.

I tried using a bin to store everyday clothes for a while, but to be honest, I hated it. It was challenging to manage, and with so many young kids, it wasn't ideal for them to dig to the bottom of the bin every day just to find a particular shirt.

The bins basically became one hash of a mess, and too cumbersome to find anything.

I went to IKEA, found a couple of decently sized dressers, had my tween/teens assemble them (a great learning moment, and dang it's kinda fun!), and assigned two drawers to each child. Boom, done. I liked it way better than the bins. The space was more shallow, but broader and easier to search through.

If you don't have space or the money for dressers, the bins are still a good option because you can fit a lot into them and, if need be, stack them up like big city skyrises.

I DO still use the square foldable bins for items like pajamas. When you have 10 kids within 17 years, you find that there are sets of kids that are close enough in age and size to share certain clothes sizes like pajamas and underwear. So we've got a couple of bins in each closet that house particular kids' PJs and underwear/socks. It works pretty well and doesn't take up their precious drawer space.

QUICK TIPS:

1. Have specified areas for all your clothing.

2. Be intentional and find a system of storage that works for you.

3. Don't regularly purchase clothes on a whim (Now and then I totally do, cause it's fun, and there's a sale. Just don't make it a habit!)

4. Less is more, generally speaking.

5. Keep what you or the kids are likely to wear within the next 6-12 months. Otherwise, "Bye, bye, collared shirt."

[8]

BATHROOM

One benefit to the girls going mostly "au natural" with our hair, make-up, and skin care is that the cosmetics and toiletries we keep in the house are minimal.

Now I don't wanna bash any genders here, but the boys' bathroom is just plain gross compared to the girls'. There, I said it. Five of our girls share one bathroom, and they manage to keep it cleaner and with less stuff than the three boys that share a bathroom. Go figure. (I'm not counting my youngest girl and boy in those numbers yet.)

> **" As far as makeup goes, we hold to an archaic practice of waiting until they're 16 years old to wear it."**

As far as makeup goes, we hold to an archaic practice of waiting until they're 16 years old to wear it. Since my girls are just starting to hit their teen years, the cosmetic and specialty products we do have are still very manageable. Hey, just one more way we can keep things simpler around here. Plus, girls are beautiful, and NOT because of make-up.

We live in a bigger house now, but after living in tight quarters for so many years, I'd adjusted to not having much storage space in the bathroom. I would hold on to an extra bottle of shampoo and conditioner, soap, and a few necessities, but rarely stocked up on toiletries.

Sharing limited bathroom space has its quirks. When we were out all day and would come home late at night, the process of getting all of us ready for bed was pretty hilarious.

"Older ones, use the main bathroom and shower first, but five minutes max for each of you then get out, pronto!"

"Oh wait, Jude needs to poop first!"

"Margot is about to pee in her pants. Hold on, Jude, you run to my bathroom. Margot get in here fast."

"No Elise, you can't go in to brush your teeth yet!"

"Alright, Margot's finished. Older ones, get your showers done!"

"Jude, are you done pooping yet 'cause I need to bathe the three youngest in my tub now."

"Oh my gosh, did Gavin seriously just go over his five minute shower allowance in the main bathroom? Gavin, GET OUT!!"

This was our story over and over. People may wonder why we left parties early. Well we had one heck of a nightly process to start if we were to finish before midnight, that's why.

We built a larger home pretty recently. All of a sudden, we found ourselves with more bathroom space than ever before. I found it funny that I didn't even know how to fill up all the cabinet space in our multiple bathrooms.

They looked sparse and lonely.

And I'm perfectly happy with that.

I've got a basket or two for brushes and hair tools in each bathroom, and a drawer with toothbrushes and toothpaste. All of the linens, towels and extra shower supplies are kept in a shared hall closet outside of both the kids' bathrooms.

Our bathrooms, like any family that has kids, can get disgustingly dirty. As far as space goes, I keep storage manageable by not stockpiling anything other than the basics — but by golly, please, Lysol wipes near every toilet and sink!

My best bet to maintaining order in these rooms is once again by taking a trash bag and going through everything, making sure empty bottles are getting thrown away, that type of thing. Putting a weekly bathroom cleaning cycle on the kids' chore list also helps with maintenance.

Now and then I'll find odd things like Twinkie wrappers in the vanity cabinet, which isn't even the craziest place I've found a food wrapper. I once unearthed a Dove Miniature ice cream bar wrapper in the toilet brush caddie, underneath the toilet brush!

What are my kids thinking? "Hmmm, Mom might see this if I walk downstairs with it. I know what I'll do, I'll lift this toilet brush up, place the wrapper, and voila! Unless she cleans our toilet, it will never be found!"

So tricky. Except sometimes I do clean their toilets, and of course I'll find the wrapper. Epic fail.

When it comes to hidden litter and attempts to sneak food, *I'm Sherlock Holmes: Mom Edition.*

For us adults, buy our favorite cosmetic and hygiene products as we need them. Nothing more, nothing less. And for goodness' sake, all that old eyeshadow from the 90's can be discarded now.

Nowadays my family's nightly routines are easier since we've gained more bathroom space. However, we still abide by a strict shower schedule. When we're coming in late from a day out, the younger kids bathe in the downstairs tub, and older girls have their own bathroom. While one child is on a five minute shower timer, the other girls brush their teeth and then switch. Same with the boys.

> **"When it comes to hidden litter and attempts to sneak food, I'm Sherlock Holmes: Mom Edition."**

QUICK TIPS:

1. Clean the bathrooms often (Or better yet, have the kids clean them!)

2. Don't overdo it on cosmetic/toiletries.

3. Kids can learn that the bathroom is not a place to spend large amounts of time. Get in, get out, carry on.

4. Get all the same colored towels. Really dark ones if you don't want to see stains, really white ones if you want to bleach them regularly

Maybe when the kids move out, their first luxury will be long showers, I dunno.

Then again, maybe they'll appreciate being trained to take short showers and limit bathroom time when they're paying for their own water, electric, and cosmetic bills.

At that point I won't care, it's their call. In my house, it's my call.

CHILD LABOR
(and Learning to Let Go of Perfection)

Sometimes people look into my life, see all the helpers that I have and think I've got it pretty good. And the truth is, I do.

But good help doesn't grow off of trees.

Much of my life as "manager of the home" has consisted of teaching the kids everyday tasks like cooking, cleaning, and picking up after themselves.

For instance:

"Okay everyone, time to clean your rooms. I want the beds made, toys put in their place, dirty laundry in the laundry room. Pull out the junk from under your bed, make sure the trash gets picked up, and wipe down those window sills. When you finish cleaning, let me know, and I'll go over it to make sure it's complete."

I set a timer, which really helps sometimes. Otherwise, kids will lollygag, get distracted and all sorts of other drama. Then I let them clean their room.

"Mom, we're done!"

I'll go in for inspection... and it looks horrible. With my all-seeing mom eyes, I'll find they mostly shuffled things around to clear a space in the middle of the floor, while the edges, nooks, and the surfaces of every piece of furniture still look messy, dusty, and in disarray.

It takes all that is within me not to 1. freak out, or 2. pat them on the back, then go through myself and quickly get it up to my standard of "clean."

It would go so much faster if I just did it myself, and let them run along and play.

But that's not what's best for them or for me. They're gonna be adults one day, and it's sorta my job to help prep them for that. So what I try to say (when it's not a PMS day) is:

"Okay, I see some progress (which is true. Everything that was in the center got moved to the edges, so yeah, progress) but there are a few things on the floor that need to be put away. And don't forget to wipe the window sills and dressers."

Insert griping, complaining, writhing bodies slumping to the ground, accusations of me being too picky, eye rolls, etc. x 10 kids.

Welcome to parenthood.

I go around and point out things they should learn to notice, give them another chance to correct them, and remind them that they won't be allowed to go play until this is done properly.

I walk away. 10-20 minutes later, I'll hear, "Mom! We're done!"

Ladies and gentlemen...

It's way improved!

I'm optimistic that with extra time and effort, my kids definitely show the capability to clean their room. It's NOT perfect, but that's okay.

This is not about creating 10 clones of me. These are kids. I choose to focus on their efforts and improvement.

And so I deem it as "well done" and let the kids run off to play. In another day or two, we'll have another chance to clean those rooms again, go over anything they missed last time, and remind them (again) how to get it right.

The kids made progress, which I choose to see as "finished."

> **"This is not about creating 10 clones of me. These are kids. I choose to focus on their efforts and improvement."**

With my personality and the priority I place on cleaning, it's sometimes hard to walk away from the room and call it "clean." I naturally want to micromanage and demand them to work until it's perfect. However, it's good for me to sacrifice some personal expectations and give others the opportunity to learn how to do it themselves (with a little bit of guidance).

Guess what? 10 kids and 17 years later, I've got some fantastic help around here.

> **"Maintaining a home with 10 kids, it's essential to always have 'all hands on deck.'"**

If I would've gone into the kids' rooms every time and nagged them to death, or cleaned it all myself, the outcome would be very different.

(To set the record straight, I do nag, my kids still think my standards for clean is too high, and all of us whine, complain, scream and cry sometimes.)

We don't have this down pat, but I have learned to let things go more for the sake of both the children's and my development. We may choose to let go of something because it would be more beneficial than holding on to it. That doesn't mean it will always feel good in the moment.

Maintaining a home with 10 kids, it's essential to always have "all hands on deck."

Kids are a lot of work, no arguing there, but they return the blessing in so many ways. Watching them enjoy life, develop, grow and learn is one of the most rewarding aspects of parenting.

Yeah, it's annoying and difficult at times to train the kids to be diligent with chores, but as the years go by, they learn personal responsibility. Eventually, life improves as we learn to function as a team.

Honestly, I can't help but be amazed at some of the ways my kids work around here. Sometimes I think, "Wow, their basic life skills around the house are pretty awesome."

A few pointers about getting kids to be more responsible and helpful around the house:

When they tell you "I can't do that" or "It's too hard," don't give in. Of course they can do it. Believe in them and give them the opportunity to become successful by practicing.

Don't let them manipulate you with laziness disguised as self-doubt! Kids will say and do whatever they can to get out of something they don't want to do.

Now when my kids tell me they're really bad at a certain task, I respond "Well then, you're the perfect one for the job!"

I admit I've given myself that excuse when I'm learning something new or taking on more responsibility, but I know, and the kids know, that's the wrong attitude to approach responsibility.

If I give them permission to give up because something doesn't come naturally or is "too hard," they may take that approach with future opportunities, and we don't want that for them as kids or adults.

Now that we have a few teenagers, Bryan and I can get away more often for a dinner out by leaving the older kids in charge.

While we were sharing a meal over a quiet table, the children stayed home and cooked an entire meal (plus dessert), cleaned up the house, and had the younger ones in bed for the evening, with everything under control.

The rewards are for real, folks! Our new reality is fantastic. It didn't happen overnight, and while it may be tiresome and inconvenient at times to let those little hands into your space, it's also worth it. Not only do you receive genuine help, but your kids find a sense of accomplishment and self-worth when they have the opportunity to both learn new things and to serve others.

> **"Mastering basic skills like household chores is often underrated in helping children develop into capable adults."**

Mastering basic skills like household chores is often underrated in helping children develop into capable adults. Don't shortchange your kids by doing it for them. Get those two-year-olds cooking and working!

QUICK TIPS:

1. Train your kids as young as possible to help out and take responsibility around the house.

2. Let them into your space, often.

3. Motivate them with kindness, but teach them that while work isn't always fun, they still have to help and "obey mommy and daddy" when they are given chores to do.

4. We don't incorporate a regular allowance for the kids. Instead, we have specific, out-of-the-ordinary jobs they can do to earn money. Regular household chores are their responsibility, and don't come with automatic payment.

5. Every Friday morning, we have a treat of iced coffee or specialty teas that all the kids can partake in, as an added "Thanks for helping out around here, kiddos." (I should note my older kids get coffee way more often than that now.)

6. GET A CHORE LIST PRINTED OUT. We use a spreadsheet of chores listed on a weekly schedule with various tasks for each kid automatically outlined. The more clear you are with kids about their responsibilities, the less stress there will be. I don't have to choose whose turn it is to take out the trash, then hear why it isn't fair. The chore list rotates, so there's no questioning whose turn it is. Boom.

7. Be patient. Be consistent. Reap the benefits.

[10]

TOYS

When you have 10 kids, toys are their own thing. And by "thing," I mean you really have to think about what you're going to do about toys.

I remember in my earlier parenting years when some of those first toys were introduced into our home and how much fun it was to get them for our little ones. I still have some of our favorites.

Over time, of course, our collection of toys started to grow. With birthdays, Christmas, generous grandparents and more kids, toys were starting to become an issue.

I decided years ago that I wasn't going to keep all the little things that come along with toys perfectly presented in adorable bins on pretty shelving. Even though I'd prefer to see everything presented in a cute and orderly manner, I realized pretty quickly that it was more work than it was worth to keep it that way.

Toys are supposed to be fun. Trying to keep them in showcase condition was only causing me stress. I gave up on that idea about three months after our second child.

But I didn't want toys overrunning the main areas of the house. I decided early on that I'd get one large toy box for the kids. All their toys (apart from say LEGOs and blocks) needed to fit inside, lid closed and all.

As we had more kids, stuffed animals was the next thing for them to collect. So when I say "one toybox," I'm not counting the stuffed animals fitting into that.

My first two kids weren't that interested in stuffed animals, but all of the others after them were. Needless to say, every birthday they wanted some variety of them. If not communicated to me, they'd mention it to their grandparents. Smart kids.

Grandma loves when the kids makes it easy on her by giving specific orders. Who doesn't? There's no need to guess how to delight a child when they just tell you straight up.

I soon realized that when you have 6-7 kids who really like these stuffed creatures, it doesn't take long to develop an "overpopulation of teddy bears" problem.

One day I gathered all the kids that had gotten into collecting beanie boos and teddy bears and stuffed whatever else, and told them "Alright, I like your collection (I truly thought I'd never like stuffed animals, but they had kind of grown on me), and I'm glad you find delight in having them, but we're gonna need to put a max number on these critters for a while."

"I want all of you to count how many you have. If we keep asking for these on every birthday, they're going to take over the house," I explained to them. "Find a nice place for them in your rooms and on your beds. Enjoy the ones you have for as long as you want, but I want you all to take a break from getting more."

> **"I shut down the stuffed animal factory. I didn't "kill" any of them, we just stopped the world over-population of them."**

Basically I shut down the stuffed animal factory. I didn't "kill" any of them, we just stopped the growing, world over-population of them.

One time, I communicated to Grandma that I didn't want the kids to get any of those life-size teddies, and that for the sake of space, let's skip that variety and move on to something different.

Grandma laughed and said "I'm glad you told me because I totally would've bought one or more for them, but I understand."

I have super awesome parents and parents-in-law like that.

It helps to communicate directly and clearly with both the kids and gift givers. It's not a personal attack, merely a practical decision that needs to be made. It also just so happens to be my preference.

Sometimes my kids are initially disappointed about a decision like this that I've made. I encourage them to let go and move on, which they eventually do.

Communicating that I understand their attachment to these things but that the family has a storage issue, it gives the kids something logical to consider, which helps with the emotional side of it.

> **"Toys are fun, but they're not the essence of a good childhood."**

Other than a plethora of teddy bears, we pretty much have the same amount of toys now with 10 kids as we did with two. One big box for the bulk collection, a couple of separate bins for blocks and legos, and a play kitchen.

You may have guessed by now that going through your collection of toys is just as necessary as going through clothes or kitchen supplies or the garden shed. There's often something broken or disgusting that can be thrown away, and it never hurts to donate a few that are still in good shape.

Pretty soon the plasticky, loudmouthed toys with sirens start getting replaced with "I just want a nice shirt, some earrings, a carving knife or some money for my birthday" anyhow.

As far as birthdays and Christmas goes, we've kept it low-key. We find a simple thing or three for each kid and that's it.

This has worked well for us. Rather than being extra stressed around the holidays, we focus more on having fun family traditions apart from toys and gifts. In short, our holidays include a little gift giving, mixed with lots of food and quality time spent together as a family.

Of course, even if I don't buy a lot of things for each kid at Christmas, it still feels like I buy a buttload of gifts. I guess that's what happens when you have a bunch of kids, huh?

QUICK TIPS:

1. Unless it's a holiday/birthday, I rarely buy toys for the kids throughout the year.

2. Most of our toys have to fit in one large toy box. I bought a fairly big toy box.

3. Toys like legos and building blocks will obviously need their own place of storage apart from the main toy box.

4. Toys are fun, but they're not the essence of a good childhood.

And the whole "cardboard-boxes-are-the-most-fun-toy-ever" sentiment really is true. I mean, when was the last time you made a fort out of boxes? It's a blast. Have you taken out a box of crayons and let the boxes become the canvas for some of the best kid art ever?

Try it. You won't be sorry.

[11]

MAINTENANCE

Maintenance is a subtle yet powerful force that, to be honest, is one of the more tedious tasks on the planet.

Can't we just let something as boring and lame as "maintenance" fall by the wayside?

I've come to realize how much maintenance has become central to how I run our home and my life.

I'm often asked "How do you do it?" or "Why are your kids so capable?" and "How are you able to homeschool on top of everything else?"

I wish I had an exciting and dramatic reply. In reality, it

comes down to a willingness to do a lot of little things many times, over and over and over.

While life has many "aha!" moments, most of our success comes from living intentionally through all of the ordinary and less "exciting" seasons of life. It sounds boring, but maintenance matters. It's absolutely vital to our existence and key to accomplishing anything in the long haul.

> **"In reality, it comes down to a willingness to do a lot of little things many times, over and over and over."**

We may get hyped about doing something and think these emotions are what drives us, but that's only the beginning. Feelings will ebb and flow. As parents, we know that parenting is one heck of a rollercoaster of emotions.

We're wired to be emotional. That's why I remind myself when starting something new with gusto that it's going to get harsh and annoying sometimes.

> **"While life has many "aha!" moments, most of our success comes from living intentionally through all of the ordinary and less "exciting" seasons of life."**

Making life work, having worthwhile relationships, and keeping our homes at least functional (if not downright pleasant) all require maintenance duties on your part.

QUICK TIPS:

1. Don't look at tedious tasks as pointless. They're often the foundation of the whole job.

2. Don't fret about how often you have to clean out the closet, again. Everyone has the same problem. Taking care of our spaces, bodies, and all of the "little stuff" is important.

3. The more space or stuff you have, the more upkeep it will require.

4. Ask yourself if the things you own are worth the investment of time you have to put into maintaining them.

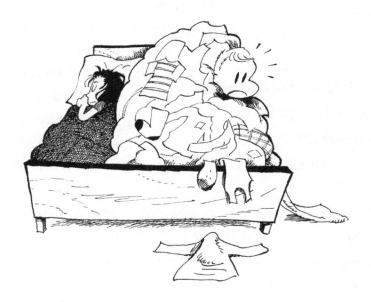

MASTER BEDROOM

There's nothing morally superior about "making your bed every day" or "not making your bed every day." However, the master bedroom is my space and it definitely sets the tone for my day.

Personally, making my bed on a near-daily basis is helpful for getting a jumpstart on all the other rooms and tasks I have that day.

I used to be a stickler about making my bed *immediately* upon waking, and NEVER leaving the house with it unmade.

In my "old age," I've given myself a little grace to get around to it when I can.

Going too many days without making my bed, however, can start to feel a bit unsettling. Almost like going too many days without a shower. It just feels good to finally get it done.

> **"'How dare the laundry defile our marriage bed?' he said."**

Some years ago I started seeing my already made bed as a great spot to throw the clean laundry if, for some reason, I didn't want it sitting in a common area. I've rarely had a "laundry room" in any of our homes, so a dedicated space other than the couch for folding laundry was usually nonexistent.

The kids and I would often end up doing it in the living room. If we had guests coming over and wanted to clear the area in a pinch, I saw my perfectly-made bed as a great place to toss the remaining laundry until I could get to it.

Yet when things are "out of sight," they easily become "out of mind." So it would happen with my laundry. I'd toss it in my room, and voila! The house was clean.

One night Bryan came home late from work and walked into our bedroom to see a mountain of clothes lying all over the bed.

"How dare the laundry defile our marriage bed?" he said.

We both laughed. (Remember, jokes and sarcasm are one of the essential "5 Love Languages" in the Orr household!)

Yet it still annoyed me to walk into my room and see our

laundry just sitting there. And it was getting to the point where Bryan was taking note as well.

His half-joking comment was just the "kick" I needed to decide laundry should stay in the common area. That way, the folding also gets done more often. Like once or twice a day. And if we go off our schedule and don't get around to it, there will be Mt. Everest to pay for.

You may have noticed by now that we function in ways that some may deem "archaic." For example, not every space in our house has to be a non-stop, open door for our kids and all of their belongings to enter.

In a life wonderfully bombarded with kids, it's nice as parents to have a space that is *mostly* ours and at least somewhat peaceful. (Let's pretend we don't know what it's like to have a screaming newborn or two sick kids sleeping with you.)

In the season of our lives when we're raising young kids, and going anywhere without them is either really difficult or doesn't happen at all, a private bedroom is a blessing. Having somewhere to retreat allows us to feel like we can connect and communicate as a married couple without leaving home.

Don't get me wrong, date nights and weekends away from home together rock, but those won't hold the two of you together for the long haul. Being intentional in your marriage, inside OR outside of the house, is where it's at.

When you can't make it happen often outside of the house, make it happen more frequently inside it.

Having a sense of privacy and peace in the master bedroom invites us into the mindset for connecting. Something as simple (but is actually hard to do) as keeping the dressers, floor and bed clear of stuff also gives us more space for conversation, focused connection, and maybe even Netflix. (Whatever your thing is.)

For our marriage, it's worth the extra effort of keeping our bedroom an in-house reprieve from the noise that is so constant (and mostly wonderful) throughout the rest of our home.

Be the master of the master bedroom. (I know, I know, that line could have multiple connotations, but you get my point.)

QUICK TIPS:

1. Make your bed. It does help set the tone in your room and everywhere else.

2. With so many years of child rearing, we like having a space that is mostly off-limits for the kids. Our bedroom is that space.

3. Honestly, if your room is a mess and that's how y'all like it, keep it up! Mess is not a sign of deficiency, it can be a personal preference. Don't you dare get all guilty up in here.

4. One way to keep the master bedroom clean is to make sure you're going through the other areas of your home and freeing up space elsewhere for everything.

[13]

DINING ROOM

Picture this: a table laden with food, chairs crowded together, people talking, laughter in the air, cups being spilled, food all over the floor, chair legs scraping back and forth, and everyone settling in for conversational dinner topics.

If that isn't what dining rooms are for, then what is it?

Sometimes it might be Thursday morning's leftover cereal bowl hidden beneath Johnny's uniform, which reeks of last Saturday's game day sweat and rotten milk from the leftover sippy cup it's lying next to. Then there are the three missing phone charging cords underneath the pile of papers that everybody has been trying to find for days.

While this table seems to be getting some practical use, it doesn't appear to be set up for meals that anyone really wants to gather for.

If that's the case, maybe it's time to clear the table.

Call me old-fashioned, but having at least one meal with everyone sitting together every day is important. If it can happen more often than that, even better.

I functioned as an avid supporter of what I saw as traditional family mealtimes until one day not too long ago I realized something:

Sail Malcolm Orr, our ninth baby had entered our lives. While we were excited to find out I was pregnant, Sail came at a somewhat crazy time in our lives. We had just begun a new construction job building a house on our seven acres of country land. Bryan had started a second business, I'd felt physically spent after baby #8, so we both discussed taking a little break from babies for awhile.

Yet life has a way of throwing your plans out the window.

Lo and behold, one day I'm like, "Waaaait a minute, I'm feeling way too pregnant not to be pregnant."

Sure enough, positive test results. In the words of artist Bob Ross: "We don't make mistakes, we just have happy accidents."

We bore through that stressful year, building our new home, with Bryan working on his main business and a little bit on his side hustle. I kept up (kind of) with the homeschooling.

I also found myself busy making all sorts of decisions for our new house. Here I was, once again, beluga-whale-pregnant in the dead heat of another Florida summer.

Sometimes I really hate Florida. Thankfully, I'm usually more positive about where we live—just not in July when I'm nine months pregnant.

The humidity and heat sucked the life right outta me.

Anyways, no pity partying here. We were about to have a brand-spanking-new home built on our property, and I wasn't going to start feeling sorry for myself.

I went into labor about five days before our scheduled move-in date. Just in time! Or was it?

I promise I don't have babies just so that people bring us meals. Yet somehow, even after all the babies we've had, friends and family still do. I'm always humbled and grateful, but this time it was EXTRA helpful.

> **"Here I was, once again, beluga-whale-pregnant in the dead heat of another Florida summer."**

We had just moved into our new house, Sail was under a week old, and Bryan realized he had a kidney stone too large to pass. So off the three of us (newborn in tow) went to an outpatient center so they could put Bryan under general anesthesia, laser explode a large kidney stone, put in a stent, and send us on our way back home.

What a week!

What does this have to do with dining rooms? I'm seriously wondering that myself.

Oh yes, so back to people bringing us meals following baby #9. The meals just kept coming. Friends and family were delivering dinners to our doorstep and man, were we grateful.

One evening, my sister Michelle came with all the goods.

She told me not to worry about a thing and just sit back while she took care of everyone's food. "If you don't mind, a couple of my kids and I will sit and enjoy dinner with you." she told me.

Michelle started serving up the plates and brought me mine, which I gratefully accepted. In my haste of eating the ridiculously tasty grub, I guess I lost sense of time.

I looked around at the table of kids finishing up their plates. Without thinking, I decided we should move on to the next activity. "Alrighty then, time to clean up. Clear your plates and cups. Move the chairs and sweep the floor underneath and around the table. Get the dining room and kitchen area cleared" I said to the children.

I glanced up to see my sister wide-eyed with mouth agape, casually walking to the table with a full plate of food in her hands. She paused and said, "Um, is this some sort of efficiency competition, 'cause seriously Leilani, I'm just getting my own plate of food... you Orrs don't waste time!"

I was embarrassed I hadn't stopped and waited until everyone, including our benevolent dinner bearer, was seated before we started to eat. Secondly, the rate at which I finished my food and started thinking ahead to the next task seemed imbalanced and unnatural.

I blame it on building a house, having a baby, and my

husband's health condition all happening at the same darn time. I was in some kind of "Must Keep Going" productive mode. My pace at the table was so ridiculous, my sister and I couldn't help but laugh. Then we sat back down to finish (her) dinner.

I needed to take a chill pill.

While I'd thought we were pretty good about traditional sit-down meals as a family, the speed at which we do it may be a little imbalanced. I think about that evening with my sister every now and then, and force myself to slow down and relax at meal time.

So, your *dining area*. While our family meals can sometimes be a bit hurried, the dining room is still an inviting place where we build positive memories. It's where we gather around to play board games; or catch up with visiting friends over midday coffee and scones, if not late night talks.

Unless we're doing a school or other short-term project, I try to keep our table cleared because I love this space to be available for gathering together.

A lot of times, the tables in our home are smack dab in the middle of common areas. People of all ages are coming and going, leaving their things on whatever surface is most convenient. If the stuff taking up space on your table doesn't have a designated spot elsewhere, just get a dang box and throw it in there. Problem solved.

QUICK TIPS:

1. I'm a stickler for clearing the table IMMEDIATELY upon finishing meals. Just get everything out of the way, pronto.

2. Enjoy this space for food, conversation, and projects if needed.

3. If you want to spark a little joy, indulge in a pretty centerpiece and make sure it's presented by itself, free of clutter. I love the simplicity of a clean dining table.

[14]

IT'S OKAY (EVEN NECESSARY) TO BE MESSY SOMETIMES

If you have kids, it doesn't hardly matter how "organized" you are, messes will still happen.

The way I manage the stress of mess is to see them as temporary. The key to not being overwhelmed is finding the distinction of messes and clutter.

Messes are much easier to deal with if the clutter has been dealt with beforehand.

That's why I talk way more about clutter than perfect organization. When you focus on and address the task of reducing things you don't need or use often, the mess can be cleaned up and put away much easier.

That's why I'm learning to welcome the mess.

I was walking to the living room couch, exhausted, at 1am in the morning. My heart was full. For two days in a row, the house had been filled with adults and children. There was so much laughter, conversation (some deeper than others), endless red solo cups, water being spilled, and dirty feet tracking through the water that had spilled.

On the floor, next to small puddles of muddy water, were remnants of the amazing flourless chocolate cake my sister had made.

And of course, there were pies. Pie crust that fell from a three-year-old's mouth and a 33-year-old's plate smashed by big and little feet trudging in and out of the house. What had once been a single piece of pie crust had magically turned into a pile of 1,000 crumbs.

The door frames were marked with handprints up and down. As I turned the knob to open the door and yell at one of the 39 kids to stop smashing the dog crate in the yard with a baseball bat, my hand stuck to goo from what I can only guess is the raspberry jello dessert I'd made.

Obviously, someone would have that all over their hands and then just run outside to play. The bathroom sink was so far away for my five-year-old nephew. I get it. Make haste, there's no time to waste.

Then there was the bathroom. When you see chocolate on the kitchen floor, you know it's chocolate. When you see chocolate smeared on the bathroom floor, the sink, and all over the light switches, it's scary because...that might not be chocolate.

Whatever toys and bikes that had been put away previously were now littered across the field. Every ball and frisbee that we owned appeared to have been tossed around. As far as the eye can see, there was a ball here, a ball there, and a ball everywhere.

Socks and shoes were thrown every which way, not placed in a row by the doorway or in a bin, of course not! There were shoes on the slide and under the trampoline and squeezed between two couch cushions and buried in the sand around the sand castle. There were one or two flip-flops in the mulch underneath the swings, because we're from the country and we like it that way.

This was the result of Thanksgiving with our families, and despite the mess, is one of the most amazing things ever. There are something like 40 grandkids on one side of the family and 21 on the other. We have so many cousins and nieces and nephews, and when the kids all get together, they know how to have a blast.

It's nothing short of deliciously fun chaos and it's really, really beautiful. For days, there is camaraderie and laughter ringing through the house, and loads of fantastic food that everybody participates in creating and consuming. It's quite an experience. You'd think I'd be used to it by now, but even I sometimes sit back in wonder.

I love it.

Being able to let order go for a short time is incredibly freeing.

Besides, like we talked about earlier, the less you have, the easier it will be to put everything back into order later.

While things may be in total disarray for pockets of time, after parties or even in our everyday life, it's always just a good cleaning and bit of organization away from exactly what it was before.

Sitting on the couch at 1 a.m. that morning after Thanksgiving, I had just finished mopping the floor and tying up loose ends around the house. The guests were gone, but before the family left, they had done their fair share of dishes, sweeping, vacuuming, and packing things up to take home with them. By the time everyone had gone, we had a mostly empty house that just really needed a good wash.

Well, by "empty house," I mean we had only 10 filthy kids that still needed baths and showers.

The time spent with our friends and family was so worth the chocolate or poop or whatever it was over the light switches.

When children enter our lives, we become aware of how much mess can happen, repeatedly and in a short amount of time.

To expect order 100% of the time is a lofty task, indeed. If you're up for that task, have at it. For me, letting kids be kids and joining in the fun is important—and sometimes that means you have to get a little messy.

There is a time and place for everything, however. I allow time in my life for the mess because there's a whole lot of beauty in the chaos if your mind is willing to notice.

Even on routine days in our house, we have plenty of messes. I don't expect surfaces to be cleared 24/7. I just make sure the kids clean up after themselves, multiple times a day if we have to.

For all I've said about minimalism, I've learned a lot from some of the messiest people I know. For one thing, they welcome you and other into their lives with open arms. They

"When children enter our lives, we become aware of how much mess can happen, repeatedly and in a short amount of time."

make you feel comfortable in your own skin, instead of worrying about every little speck of dust or dirt. They let kids be kids. You never have to worry whether they'll be shocked when your kid has an accident and pees all over the floor.

I want to be the kind of person that can let things go, just another fallible human being who embraces the messy accidents of real life and allows others to do the same.

It doesn't mean you have to let your house and yard go to pot all the time, but make space for inconveniences and mess in your life. It's worth it!

QUICK TIPS:

1. Mess is a part of life and creativity, embrace it.

2. We have a 10 minute "G.P." (general pick-up) process that I adopted from my own childhood. When I say "Do G.P.," the kids tackle messes in the common areas and have learned to clean it all up in 10 minutes or less.

3. Mess isn't so stressful when you focus on tackling it at an appropriate time, and allowing yourself to relax in the meantime.

4. If you're having a big party, get extra clutter cleared away beforehand. That way, it will be a lot easier to clean up after a party. (It sounds backwards, but it's true. If your party starts out clean, it'll be easier to tackle the clean-up later.)

5. Let kids be messy, but don't feel bad about reminding them to clean up after themselves. Ditch the "mom guilt" about being too "naggy." Someday your children (and their future spouses) will thank you.

YES, I STILL HAVE FUN!
(And How to Find More Time)

I think one of the misconceptions people may have about "orderliness," "structure," "routine" and "responsibility" is that they don't leave much room for spontaneity.

COMPARED TO WHAT?!

Letting go of "must-do's" and finding time for recreation is essential to incorporate into our lives. Being too tied down to work, routines, and appointments will eventually take its toll and drain the life right out of our existence.

We're made to enjoy things. To notice the beauty around us. Not to micromanage every moment of our lives.

We have 24 hrs. every single day. Like many people, you may feel like you're always running out of time. I really believe that if you get better at managing your time, you'll see that time doesn't control us. We can be lord over time!

One reason I enjoy having structure, saying "no," and making sacrifices is so I can make space to say 'yes" in other areas, like accomplishing goals that are meaningful AND fun. It's helped me see that when I'm intentional, I have WAY MORE TIME than I previously thought.

We waste so much time losing our heads over not having time to do anything, when really if we'd just shut our whining mouths up for a minute and take a deep breath and jot down what it is we actually want to accomplish, we see that we do have time to do those "fun" things after all.

I'm guilty as anyone of using the phrase, "I just don't have the time." I mean, having 10 kids is sort of an acceptable get-out-of-jail-free card. I sure as heck know I put off stuff and tell myself that I'm too overwhelmed to be able to do this or that. What I'm really saying when that happens is that I am making the choice to "let life happen to me" rather than "doing what it takes to make life happen."

This brings me to a quote from beloved author, Jon Acuff:

"Choose what to bomb. You can't be amazing at everything. You get to decide what matters most, and choose the things you won't worry about."

Let go of the misconception that having structure and being purposeful means you have to let go of all fun and/

or spontaneity. In my opinion, having structure just helps you become more aware of the choices you're making, what you're focusing on and what you're "bombing."

For someone like me who values routine and structure (but still craves spontaneity now and then) the mindset of "saying no" without guilt, is extremely liberating. I can live my everyday, ordinary life and sprinkle it with the extraordinary or frivolous activities as I see fit.

For instance, have you ever been camping in a tent with kids?

We pushed, we crammed, and with very little breathing room left, we somehow shut the back doors on our 15 passenger van.

The supplies we packed for our five-day camping trip made it look like we were moving to another state for life. You'd never guess I had tried to "pack light."

So we rolled up to the campground, got the number for our reserved lot, and meandered down the narrow campground road to site #23. Water bottles, two pacifiers, a dozen loose pieces of beef jerky, five shoes and three books tumble out the side door as almost all our kids push and shove to exit the van at the same time.

Sometimes, just getting out of the vehicle can be a long and strenuous adventure.

I wander around the site to scope out an area for our tents and started to feel a little concerned. We had not one, but TWO tents to set up and our van alone was already taking up the entire length of the site.

There was no room for both of our tents and our vehicle. The campground was filling up fast around us. I didn't know what to do.

It looked like maybe the site across from us was still available, but it wasn't much bigger. We made a quick call up to the ranger's office.

"Campgrounds are breeding grounds for weirdos."

"Is the site across from #23 available for the length of our stay? We're having a little bit of an issue with space and want to rent out both sites."

"It's filling up fast here, but let me check," said Ranger Rick.

"Okay, it looks like that's the only site left in your loop."

Omg! "Okay, I'll take it!"

"You're going to need to come up front and pay right away. The sites that aren't reserved are first come, first serve."

"Bryan, get the heck down there, we gotta get the second site. I'll put our tents up on one site, and we can park our van across the street at the other site."

You have to understand that at this time, our kids were all under the age of 13. There was no way I was going to separate our tents, in a packed campground, on the beach, in Florida.

Campgrounds are breeding grounds for weirdos.

Some might say we're pretty weird. I mean, who decides to camp with eight kids under the age of 13?

But the weirdos I'm talking about are the 58-year-old-men who walk around shirtless in pajama pants to the shared bathrooms at 11 p.m., then stop on the road to chat with the wild raccoons coming out of the woods.

So anyway, while Bryan books it to the front office and snags that other site, I start setting up our tents.

Bryan doesn't generally like camping in Florida because of the humidity, heat, and pests. Somehow, I convinced him to try it again this year.

We normally take a family road trip up north, but this year we were putting the plans for our house together and our vacation funds had all been allocated to the building project. Feeling like our family still needed a break from the mundane, I decided we should camp at the local beach here in Florida, where it would cost next to nothing.

As I'm putting up the tents, Bryan comes back with a confirmed reservation for the site across the street. We park the van and camp kitchen stuff at one site and set our tents up at the other.

The week turned out to be interesting. The campground was infested with raccoons that kept getting into our neighbors' coolers and tearing up their sites. You'd think they would've figured out to put food away in their vehicle.

You should have heard the racket next door two nights in a row. I thought a site with eight kids was loud, but this small family next door was up at all hours of the night freaking out at the raccoons.

The critters weren't even phased, but continued tipping coolers, opening lids, throwing cans and making their high-pitched grunting sounds while the humans were fighting with each other and trying to chase the raccoons with a broom. As soon as the human family went back inside their tent, the racoon family came right back.

No, they weren't rabid raccoons. They were just ridiculously good at thieving campsites where people are silly enough to leave food out.

The family next to us finally gave up and left the campground in the middle of the second night there. My guess is, they decided to finish their "vacation" elsewhere.

I felt kinda bad for them.

Meanwhile, we were over here having so much fun sweating, getting eaten by sand fleas, taking eight kids to the beach, then coming back to the dirty campground bathrooms and trying to get all the salt and sand washed out of our hair before bed.

Then there were the midnight walks to the bathrooms with multiple groups of toddlers who all needed to pee "real bad."

Those walks are fun.

You'd hear rustling in the woods and wonder what the heck you were going to see next

Oh, no biggie, just a lost drunk person looking for his campsite and waving just a little too friendly at you.

I pulled the kids close and hurried to the well-lit bathroom. So well-lit that the dirt, spider webs, bugs, grimy walls, and dirty toilets were all clear and easy to see.

When we finally got back to our tent, I hoped to finally catch some shut-eye; it had been difficult to do the first couple of nights with the aggressive raccoons-and-human arguments next door.

Bryan, lucky him, can sleep like a rock through this sort of thing. This was one of those times I really wished I had the same ability.

I unzipped the tent door, stooped inside, tripped on 10 pair of flip flops, and plopped down onto the air mattress.

Then I hear another, "Mom, I gotta go pee."

Oh my gosh!

Bryan mutters something. He did actually hear us, go figure!

"I'll take him," Bryan said, and off the next group goes.

Despite all that crazy, of course, we also had a blast.

We got to play in the waves, roast marshmallows and hot dogs around a fire, made pancakes in the morning and sipped on good coffee. (I try not to go anywhere without good coffee. One reason our van was so packed is that I insisted on bringing an extension cord and our 12 cup coffee maker.)

I watched as the kids alternated between sibling fun and rivalry. We drove around the local town and did all the touristy things we could think of. The kids spun around (and around, and around) the campground loop on their scooters and bicycles.

We had good memories on that trip, and ended up having a lot of fun. It was also a lot of work, but that's camping/parenting for you.

Our family manages to have fun in all sorts of situations. It's just a matter of mindset. You can have an expensive, luxurious trip planned, but if it's peppered with expectations and disappointment, you may not even enjoy it.

Camping with even two, much less 10, kids can be a horrible

experience, but if you embrace the difficulties, you'll have a blast.

Make time in your life to do "fun" things. What those are will look different for each of us. If camping is not your thing, pick a different activity.

Don't get stuck in the mentality that you don't have time for things that get you out of your everyday routine. You do have time.

QUICK TIPS:

1. When you truly analyze your schedule, you'll likely see you have more time than you thought. Don't waste that time with self-induced "I don't have the time" falsehoods.

2. Be courageous and try something new! (Camping will not be "fun" for everyone, but it can be an experience of a lifetime.)

3. One of the fab things about having structure is that you can actually see where and when you "need" to fit in responsible stuff while allowing spontaneity elsewhere.

4. I've arranged our homeschooling schedule to four-day school weeks year round (skipping the two-month summer break) because this gives me a three-day weekend EVERY WEEK. Now I have the option to spontaneously take the kids to the springs as I see fit.

5. This may sound boring to the younger party crowd, but over time I've started seeing projects as opportunities for fun. It may not carry the same vibe as a beach day, or ladies' night out, but there's something pretty awesome about making progress on something cool. (Sometimes my kids agree, sometimes not.)

$\begin{bmatrix} \mathbf{16} \end{bmatrix}$

HOMESCHOOLING

As someone who often tosses important papers accidentally while trying to free up storage space, technology was the best thing that ever happened to me.

Sure, a physical book in your hands still has a wonderful feel that an iPad or tablet will never replace, but going paperless has been liberating for both my homeschooling methods and my filing cabinets.

As a homeschooler, it can be a real issue finding space for all the books, old projects, science tools, reports, folders, pens, pencils, erasers, markers, crayons — and, homeschooling parent or not, the silly pictures your toddlers draw up and hands to you 358 times a day.

Especially the drawings where arrows are flying, and blood is coming out of everyone's body. Then your kid will point to the sketch of you in the corner. It'll be the figure with the long face, with one of its eyes on the chin, the other is on "your" forehead, and hair poking out at non-symmetrical angles.

But there'll be a heart around that sketch of "you," and your kid will say something sweet like "Mommy look, it's you getting me cereal for breakfast!"

Maybe they don't even say something nice, but there's still a heart, and it's your kid's artwork and you know they're going to ask to see it again next week.

"Mommy, where's that one picture I drew for you?"

Then there are school books. I haven't completely gone paperless with our homeschool resources. We use a mixture of online courses and actual textbooks. And we definitely like to have actual paperback books on hand for us to read.

But what do we do with all this stuff?

For the first 10 years of homeschooling our kids, I didn't have a dedicated room and or storage space for school items. My solution was to install a number of cheap bookshelves anywhere I could find space for them.

That meant shelves in the dining room corners, the living room, and even one in the bedroom (well, the only bedroom that had space for it).

And then I gave each child a 16" x 11" bin, which the kids would use to store their notebook, workbooks, and a small case for pencils/erasers. We'd stack the bins in two towers, three bins high, underneath the one desk that we had in the living room. I also had a spare bin for extra supplies like pencils, erasers and science experiment gadgets.

Every morning when it was time to start schoolwork, each of my "students" would bring their bin into the dining area (yes, we did school work at the dining table) and work out of their box. As the lunch hour came around, we'd simply put everything back in the bin, scoot them aside, and set the table up for lunch.

All of the novels, biographies, textbooks, and various recipe books we used were stored on those bookshelves scattered throughout the house. For easier access, we kept the books we used more often in the dining area bookshelves because that's where we did our studying.

> **"The books made me feel educated, even when I'd have a lapse in memory and confuse the 15th century with ancient history."**

I really liked how the books in every room looked.

They made me feel educated, even when I'd have a lapse in memory and confuse the 15th century with ancient history.

Being the great mom and home educator that I am, I'd be discussing some historical moment with my 10-year-old. He'd get this quizzical look on his face and say something like, "Um, mom, what are you talking about? That was closer to

Christopher Columbus's time, what I'm talking about was during the Achaemenid Empire with Alexander the Great in 300 BC..."

Whatever.

My kid wasn't named Alex for nothing.

I'd say something stupid like "Ha! Just testing you to see if you were paying attention."

I'd inwardly blame my memory lapse on postpartum or pregnancy or PMS or something else. Pretty soon, I'm going to need to find a new card to play.

Having our school area be the same space as the eating area wasn't always ideal.

First of all, you can imagine what the table looks like in the morning after a buttload of pancakes, eggs, and bacon have been consumed by my army of children.

More often, it's a breakfast of cold cereal, but let's use the big breakfast for dramatic effect here. Bits of pancake riding down cascades of maple syrup to the floor. Runny eggs and their yolky ways sliding off the edges of the table and under our feet. The air permeated with greasy, frying bacon (This was before I started baking the bacon, which is way easier and a little healthier. Duh!)

When I'd go to clear plates and forks, they'd be so sticky I couldn't get them off my fingers to throw into the sink. Sippy cups would be on their side dripping milk (even though they're not supposed to leak) which, of course, finds its way down to the floor to join the syrup, soggy pancakes, and globs of egg yolk.

Following this, we now have 15 minutes to clean up, grab our books and bring everything to this same table to start school like the "organized" big family that we are.

It's interesting how working in imperfect circumstances gives you the opportunity to analyze your routines and get them down to a practical, works-for-you, science.

Our system became the norm, though we've had to make adjustments as the family grew even as our living space did not. All of us have circumstances in our lives that you just learn to work around.

After years of sharing our school table with our dining area, the first thing I did when we finally built our home was plan a dedicated "school room", but with some extra thought I realized I'd actually grown *to like* doing school work in a common area.

We were planning to have our classroom towards the back of our new house, in a quiet hallway so the kids could focus. Suddenly, it seemed cold, inconvenient and out of the way of life itself.

Yet I couldn't forget how annoying and inconvenient it was to repeatedly shut our books, shuffle things off the dining room table, and put everything back into a bin just to eat.

We could never leave a puzzle or creation out because two hours into school, and it'd be time for lunch when the kids would make yet another heck of a mess on our school table.

I had a few options for this room as we planned our new house, but I needed to make a decision about how I wanted to prioritize our school space.

Instead of a room off the end of some hall, I decided to make a space off the front foyer that would have rows of dedicated built-in shelves for our books. For a workspace, I planned to have someone build a couple of pull-down "Murphy" style tables that could be stowed back in the wall when the kids weren't using them. These would be nestled among the built-in bookshelves in the front hall.

> **"A few sketches a year from each child are precious. Filing 17 of them every day isn't gonna happen with this mama."**

I had a whole vision for how our school area would look. When the tables were folded into the wall, I wanted them disguised as faux cabinets on either side of the bookshelves. On the wall behind the Murphy tables, I'd have a few shelves for the ugly-looking stuff like tape, glue, crayons, and staplers.

The tables would pull down into a large front hall open the kitchen, dining, and living areas. I would keep fold-up chairs in a closet and set them up each morning for school.

It would have enough space for eight students, smack dab in the middle of all of the stuff I'd be doing when I'm not sitting with them— like cooking, cleaning, entertaining the two toddlers, and nursing a baby.

That set-up is working for us beautifully. It's simultaneously in the middle of everything and completely its own workspace.

When school is out and we have people over, we fold the

tables back into the wall and it just looks like a finished wall with cabinets and shelves of books.

Had I not been "inconvenienced" by homeschooling my kids for years at the dining room table, I wouldn't have known how much I liked teaching our children in the thick of it all.

Even now with all the dedicated space we created for school supplies and books, we still find items pile up if left unattended to.

Once again, I grab that handy trash can. Every month or so, the kids and I will go through the school cabinets and clean them out, throwing away sketches and any paper items we no longer need.

Of course, I can't keep every single piece of art my 10 children make for me over the years. It would be enough to wallpaper my whole house. I'll usually pick one or two pieces here and there. I have a large manilla envelope for each child with important documents, and I file their special sketches in those.

A few sketches a year from each child are precious.

Filing 17 of them every day isn't gonna happen with this mama.

QUICK TIPS:

1. Take time out to plan where everything should go.

2. The natural way to homeschool is to allow for some flexibility. After all, that is one of the benefits of not attending a conventional school. While there are days we move about (sometimes outside, sometimes the living room), we also have a set space and time that we begin studying. You'll feel less chaotic and more focused if you begin with some semblance of order before allowing changes.

3. Clean out old school supplies regularly. There's no need to hold onto years and years of workbooks and papers. Toss 'em.

4. While I detest bins for clothes storage, they are great for workbooks and papers.

[17]

MORE OR LESS (SPACE), IT WILL GET FILLED

Over the years, I've lived in homes of many different sizes. I've come to realize that no matter how much space or number of kids we have, every house can easily become chaotic.

I used to think that if I had a bigger house, keeping it tidy wouldn't be so hard. Any preconceived notions I had have been thrown out the window.

Of course, more space gives me flexibility in some areas and makes some things easier. For the most part however, it just comes down to addressing clutter regularly to keep messes in check.

I remember laughing inwardly when friends would tell me, "The bigger the house, the more work it's going to be for you."

I thought it'd be funny if they were to trade places with me for a while. They could try living with 11 people in 1,500 square feet. Maybe then they'd stop saying silly things like "more space is more work."

I'm embarrassed to say it, but my friends were kinda right.

In my little space when the bedrooms and central areas and two small bathrooms were tightly connected, it was easy to put things away. You just took a few steps, and everything was within reach. I also knew where everyone was, and what messes were happening throughout the house.

In a smaller home, everything is right before your eyes. Now that I have an upstairs, I can easily

"I used to think that if I had a bigger house, keeping it tidy wouldn't be so hard. Any preconceived notions I had have been thrown out the window."

ignore the rooms that aren't right in front of me. If I'm not double-checking that the kids are keeping their rooms in order, those spaces can quickly become a horrifying sight.

Of course, there are wonderful things about having more space, especially now that we have a dozen people living together. The main difference is that life has become more comfortable.

As far as stuff goes, however, I function exactly the same as I did when we lived in a doublewide trailer. If we're not going through clothes and toys and trash regularly, the generous closet and room spaces can easily get disastrous, just as before. It may take longer for the results to show, but it builds up just the same.

QUICK TIPS:

1. Don't think that more space will solve your stuff problems. Stuff is problematic no matter how much room you have.

2. Toss your stuff, y'all. Regularly. I don't always know exactly how it accumulates, but it does, so have a toss bin or bag handy at all times. Then stop buying stuff unless you have the space or the need.

3. More space won't make you happier.

4. More stuff won't make you happier.

[18]

GRIT
(Because It's Worth It!)

It seems pretty natural to look at the success of others and want in on their "secret."

When I look at my journey as a parent and homemaker, so little of my achievements had anything to do with natural talent, having money, or being especially intelligent.

For instance, as a kid, I hated cooking. I'd happily clean and organize rather than put a meal on the table. Being in the kitchen just felt like a drag. My mom, being a good parent, insisted that I learn at least some basic cooking skills, even if I didn't like it.

At her encouragement, I found a recipe for coffee cake. If you remember, I was that kid who earned $5 and couldn't wait to buy junk food with it. The same youngster who would eat a stick of butter at the kitchen table when I was four years old, or sneak into the pantry and gobble down the butterscotch chips mom saved for her cookies.

I remember slathering mayo on bologna, sandwiched between two pieces of horrible, no good for you, deliciously white Wonder bread. It happened pretty often.

No wonder I now hate both mayo and butterscotch chips. Apparently, as a kid, I had a hard time knowing when to stop.

I still really like butter though. Go figure.

Anyways, I loved food but hated cooking.

Because mom said I needed to practice my kitchen skills, I found this coffee cake recipe and decided I would have a go at it. To be honest, I was more driven by my desire to eat coffee cake than learning to be a great baker.

I tried the recipe, and it was good. All my siblings liked it, too. I remember basking in their accolades. I decided then and there that I was going to make that coffee cake more often.

It required a sponging period of an hour or more, plus a baking time of 50 minutes. If I wanted to have it ready for breakfast, I'd have to wake up really early.

I remember setting my alarm for 5 a.m. to work on my special recipe. Growing up in a large family, there was something magical about being in the kitchen all by myself for two hours before the sun rose. Now that I think about it, that may have been how I became a morning person.

On top of the fact that a lot of people were going to enjoy the thing I was making. It also dawned on me that cooking wasn't all bad.

I had a delightful time becoming known for my coffee cake and Danish (another recipe I found, and later mastered).

Fast forward to my life now, with 10 kids of my own. There's a whole lot of cooking going on around here.

I still don't much care for the art of cooking, but I do find things about it that make it worthwhile and sometimes even enjoyable. The nourishment of food, the flavors, the fact that I can save money by making things at home, and the reality that it's a necessity to keep the people I love alive and healthy.

With that motivating me, I became intentional with cooking, and have attained a certain measure of "success" in the kitchen—none of it due to my natural talent. This fact of cooking talent, or lack thereof is often brought to my attention, like when I tried out a new recipe recently:

The kids, Bryan, and I were all sitting at the table eating together. We're tasting and analyzing the flavor, when Bryan turns to me and says, "Honey, what can I do to make you taste test while you cook?"

"Nothing," I reply. "I don't like checking how something tastes while I'm making it. That's why I follow a recipe. Someone else is supposed to do that job."

"I understand, but this could've been easily tweaked just by trying it and see what it lacks," he responds.

"Well dear, I guess I'll leave that art of cooking for you on your Friday night dinners," I told him.

Clearly, natural talent isn't something I have in the kitchen. The good thing is, more what determines success is being intentional and practicing, a lot.

The moment you realize that, the world is full of opportunity!

DON'T ALLOW EMOTIONS TO BE YOUR RULER:

Emotions. They're powerful and ever changing.

Positive and negative emotions play a big part in how we experience life and our relationship with others around us.

They can sway you into decisions that may seem "wonderful" one moment and "horrifying" the next. We're wired to experience, to deal with, and to express our emotions.

They can be glorious, but also terribly misguided.

I can't tell you the amount of times I've told the kids, Bryan, or myself in periods of struggle that, "There is nothing wrong with feeling these emotions, but we shouldn't base our choices and reactions on emotion alone."

I'm often faced with the way I feel and what I believe deep down to be right and true. Sometimes they go together, while other times they're in conflict.

One of the greatest reminders I can give myself during moments of anger, anxiety, or fear is that emotions don't define my situation or who I am. I stand on what I believe, not how I feel. I start telling myself the truth, the good things, the "why" behind what I do and who I am.

When I step back from an intensely emotional moment in my life and give it time to settle before reacting, I can "see" situations with more clarity and a better perspective.

We've all made emotional decisions based on how we felt in the moment, sometimes for the better. When I think about "positive" emotional decisions I've made, it took something stronger than just the excited feeling I get from a new diet, relationship, huge project, having a baby, starting a business, etc.

Having a rational foundation for the goals you set for yourself is fundamental to sticking with them for the long haul.

FOCUS

I've had people ask if raising a bunch of kids, homeschooling, and the routine of life without having a career is boring.

Well, that's up to the person doing it!

Sure, the stay-at-home parent life can get 'boring,' but so can a career, or a purely recreational life where you don't have to work.

There are so many things we can accomplish, learn and enjoy, wherever we are.

For example, there's always something I can be working on as a mom. If you're a parent, you know how often kids need *something*.

If I'm bored, it's likely my mindset that needs adjusting, not my life.

Focus is something that I believe every person can benefit from. When you have something to work towards, there's nothing boring about existing.

I won't sit here and pretend here that I've never felt aimless.

"If I'm bored, it's likely my mindset that needs adjusting, not my life."

There are days, seasons even, when I've felt totally 'out of whack' and overwhelmed.

Yet relying on those feelings to describe my reality doesn't serve me. They may be tough to navigate, I wake up every morning, consider the opportunities before me, and remind myself that I'm a mom. The position is challenging, sure, but also incredibly rewarding and cool.

It goes without saying that I have a mentor. I go to God a lot. My faith in Him is the rock on which I stand. As I've found my identity in Him, there is a great comfort even when I may feel lost and overwhelmed on my own. He is able to guide and to hold and give me all the strength I need for the responsibilities at hand.

Focus on what the day or week holds for you. (Hopefully, you can do this over some coffee!)

Your life is like a canvas, and every step within the bigger picture is another brushstroke of the artwork being created all around you.

Staying *focused* has played a big part in my roles of parenting and managing our home. It doesn't mean I'm always strong, have a smile on my face, or am even a good person. It's about walking through the weaknesses, the setbacks, the flaws and embracing our realities with joy.

Whenever I am bombarded with scattered thoughts,

expectations, and inconvenient circumstances, giving myself space to separate from the moment before I react has helped a lot. Remembering to respond with more vision has been a beautiful strengthening exercise for me.

It's not about denying that I struggle. Sometimes all I feel in the moment is that life sucks, or that I want to find a dark cave, eat a whole pint of gelato by myself, and stay there for the rest of my life.

No biggie, don't fret about those emotions.

Be courageous. Recognize those dark feelings, but move forward with a vision of hope for what lays ahead of you. And *please don't become a cave-dwelling hermit for too long.*

Addressing our negative emotions and habits, and combating them with truth and love strengthens you. Hope becomes much closer and a part of who you are.

Those dark moments and seasons can begin to come less frequently and for shorter periods of time.

Whether those periods last 45 seconds or two years, you'll reap wonderful rewards staying the course and continuing to sail through the tumultuous waters. The storm will always let up. Don't miss out on the amazing beauty and peace that awaits you on the other side.

DON'T WALLOW IN SELF-PITY

Self-pity. It's debilitating. There's nothing beneficial about it. It can ruin your life, and drag others down with you. Just stop. I'm serious. Otherwise, you'll get stuck and burrow deeper and deeper into that very muddy pit(-y).

Self-pity is extremely destructive. It lies to your soul. It robs you of joy, halts progress and provides no value to your or anybody else's life. No matter how much you think pouting will make you feel better, it will never do you any good.

Even if life is difficult, self-pity isn't going to help you out of that hardship.

Move on. Put your big girl pants on, take your eyes off of yourself and go help someone else. It's counterintuitive, but the times you want to stay home and wallow is exactly when you need to focus on others. Interacting selflessly with others will encourage you to find some perspective.

Help someone else, and you'll be happier. Go figure.

PARENTING IS REWARDING

As I write this, tears are welling up in my eyes.

Whatever difficulties you experience as a parent, or is going on in your kids' lives, remember this:

They are worth the fight. You are their warrior.

As parents, we show up every day to do all the "little" things nobody appreciates. Wiping up the milk again and again, teaching them kindness and respect, doing yet another load of laundry, listening to sibling conflict, training your child to clear his plate (and dealing with the temper tantrum that follows).

Bearing through our emotions of inadequacy, frustration, boredom, and insignificance.

I am undeserving of the gift of being a mom. Parenting is a rewarding and ridiculously beautiful opportunity that has been set before us.

It may not be glamorous or flashy.

It happens in the subtle moments between comforting those who are hurt, helping them learn, watching the childlike joy in your kids as they stumble around, exploring the world around them.

It happens when you're holding and caring for a helpless newborn. Then as the moments turn to days, and days to years, all of a sudden your baby is nearly an adult on a path of their own unique and wonderful journey.

How can we ever believe the lies we tell ourselves that *the little things we do as parents and managers of our homes amount to nothing?*

This is why it's so beneficial to take the opportunity given to you, and embrace it fully, right now. Every day. For as long as it takes.

I say this from experience. You won't regret the moments where you sacrifice convenience and ease for the sake of love.

BUCK-UP

I do have one more "hard-to-swallow" pill, and it's one I take all the time. I'm not trying to force it on you, but if you want to know the pills I'm taking, this is one of them:

"Buck-Up" is full of Vitamins P and V! (See what I did there?)

We live in a wonderful era when we are all able to express our feelings and emotions fully, and be accepted for them. We hear a lot more talk about "giving yourself grace and space" than our parents, or their parents before them, and

> **"My life as a mother to 10 kids sometimes calls for serious "get over yourself" medicine. And I'll tell you what, it doesn't always taste good."**

I believe that's a genuinely good thing.

But that doesn't mean we don't have to buck up a whole lot and get gritty.

I don't say "buck up" to be harsh. I say this to myself and the ones I care about most because I know deep down that it serves us well.

My life as a mother to 10 kids sometimes calls for serious "get over yourself" medicine. And I'll tell you what, it doesn't always taste good.

I don't think you have to be a mom of 10 to relate. I think most people know what it's like to feel overwhelmed and have little desire to go forward.

We need rest and refreshment to feed our bodies and souls, but we also become stronger when we allow the stretching, pulling, and working out of our problems to tone us up. The strength we build helps us face our problems and move on from them, instead of running away.

Giving up because "we just can't" doesn't work when you've got three kids grabbing your ankles.

Since we can't just "throw up our hands and walk out the door," what's the next step?

Be a problem solver:

- Pinpoint your perceived "problem" and start figuring out ways to help solve it, one step at a time. (The same way we ate that elephant!)
- Make some changes in your schedule. (Remember, you say "no" so that you can say "yes" somewhere else.)
- Dedicate time to spend with your spouse or another adult.
- Take 10-minute "breathers" from the kids throughout the day. If you can't find 10 minutes, try two minutes, or 30 seconds, whatever it takes.
- If necessary, eat a pint of gelato.

Use your break wisely. Enjoy it. Refresh. Re-focus. Be grateful that you have "so much on your plate" and get back in the game come Monday (or realistically, in 5 minutes).

You'll get through it. And the more grateful you are, the more light can shine in on your circumstances.

Pretty soon you won't have to "run away" to find peace. You'll be able to rest right where

> **"We need rest and refreshment to feed our bodies and souls, but we also become stronger when we allow the stretching, pulling, and working out of our problems to tone us up."**

you are, in the here and the now, amidst the battles and the hardship, because all of it is part of your beautiful life story.

Look at the problems at hand more as opportunities than personal attacks.

Simplifying our homes and how we think or respond are all steps in the pursuit of bringing order into a chaotic life. It's not about perfection by any stretch of the word.

Remember, you can always have what you want when you choose to want what you already have.

Find your groove, get gritty, and buck up y'all.

●

The Orr Dozen

Made in the USA
Monee, IL
20 December 2020

54398161R00080